Rosario
Yesterdays
A Pictorial History

by
Christopher M. Peacock

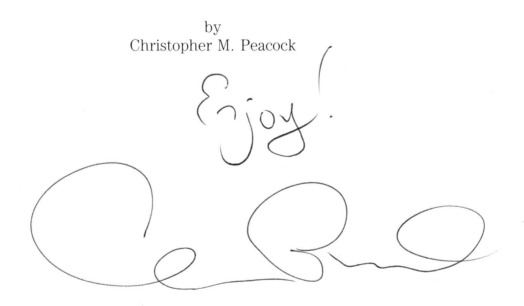

Enjoy!

Published by Rosario Productions

Afternoon Tea on the veranda with croquet on the lawn — Rosario, Orcas Island, Washington— 1911.

(courtesy of Rosario Resort)

Cover photo — Moran Mansion
(by Matthew Neal McVay)

Library of Congress Catalog Number: 85-51170

ISBN: 0-9614970-0-9

Production and printing by ADPRO Litho

Printed in the United States of America

To the Geiser family,
who have made Rosario a
place for all to enjoy.

Robert Moran's son Malcolm with adopted sister Mary. "We discovered that we could create something of a stir with old lady visitors by carrying on our end of the following conversation: 'What nice children! I suppose you are twins.' 'No ma'am; my sister's a month and a half older than I am.' That evidently gave them food for thought and fuel for imagination."

(courtesy of Rosario Resort)

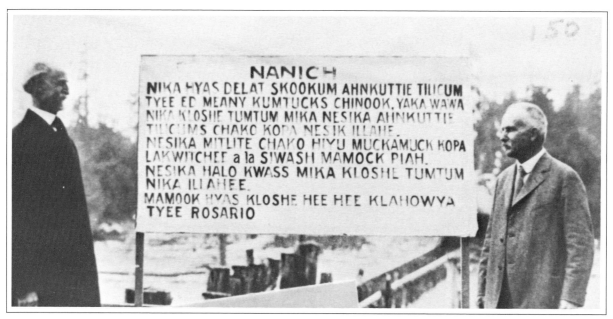

Moran welcomes his good friend, Prof. Edmond Meany of the University of Washington, to Rosario. The sign is written in Chinook jargon, the local Indian dialect which is a mixture of the native, French, and English language. Roughly translated it reads: ATTENTION! My very true long time friend Chief Ed Meany understands Chinook. I welcome you my long time friends to our place. We're going to have a big feast over Indian fire. I'm not shy to welcome you to our place. We'll have a lot of fun. Greetings, Chief Rosario.

(courtesy of Betty Moran Burns)

Contents

Introduction

Rosario — Orcas Island, Washington.   (courtesy of Rosario Resort)

Rosario, the palatial estate of Seattle ship-builder Robert Moran, sits overlooking Cascade Bay on Orcas Island in the San Juan Archipelago. The massive, elegant Moran mansion, centerpiece of Rosario, faces a beautiful panorama of blue water, evergreen forests and distant islands.

The building of Rosario was a gigantic project, planned by a man who loved to build and build to endure. Called the "Showplace of the San Juans" and "San Simeon of the Northwest," Rosario was simply the continuancy of Moran's "lifelong urge to be continually pushing ahead on industrial construction work."

The Moran mansion itself reflects pure architectural ideas emphasizing the shipbuilder's sound nautical engineering experience. This unique architectural style is most visible in the building's interior. Architectural interiors are expressions determined by the values and life style of the occupants, and for this reason, some of the best interior design is done by individuals for themselves, as with Moran. He used the finest shiprights available to craft the finest materials, personally supervising the design and quality construction throughout the mansion. It is written that art and architecture are a "bringing together of land and man out of respect, honor and celebration," and the success of this union is evident throughout the estate. Moran's interiors were kept simple and durable, for he believed "at Rosario you view the outside beauties of nature."

Part of Rosario's charming appeal lies with Orcas Island itself. The people who make passage to the island are often searching for quiet beauty, and a time to reflect on this peaceful coexistence of man and nature. There is something in an island. The dreams we have about them, the reality they are — they express the very heart of contemporary longing for definition, self-expression and security. There is no doubt that island living, on any island, is enchanting. Adding to this enchantment, local folklore includes islanders sprinkling flour on their floor to catch the imprints of the fairies who call on them at night, for magic is in the air they breathe. Whether the islander is an old timer, or a new adventurer wondering about, everyone is part of an arcadian atmosphere which reminds one of Sir Isaac Walton and his words "Praise God, be quiet and goe a'fysshgnge."

Through his 1939 autobiography, written when he was 82, and through his great love of photography, Robert Moran has helped shape our vision of that period of Northwest history.

An Address by Robert Moran, which appears throughout this volume, was delivered at the Fiftieth Jubilee Meeting of the Pioneers Association of the State of Washington on June 6, 1939 in Seattle. Moran was elected President of the association for that year, and in honoring him the Pioneers Association had honored itself. He was truly one of the great figures in Northwest history, and through his strength in character and pioneering courage, he brought renown to Seattle and the State of Washington for many years. Called the "Andrew Carnegie of the Northwest" and the "Fairy Godfather of the San Juans," the very fact of being so far from his native New York City stamped him as a man possessed by both initiative and resource. No career in Pacific Northwest annals so well illustrates the importance of individual achievement. Moran hoped his autobiography would be "helpful to younger men who need inspiration in an age of uncertainty."

The Moran photograph collection contains over 600 plate glass slides from the late 1800's and early 1900's, taken not only by Moran himself, but also by Pacific Northwest pioneer photographer Asahel Curtis. The Curtis photographs were published in 1932 in an album entitled *Rosario: An Estate in the Pacific Northwest*, designed by Moran for the sale of his estate.

Today, the shipbuilder and his mates are replaced by tourists, for Rosario has become one of the most popular resorts in North America. But when visitors step into the Moran mansion, they can't help but reflect on a different time in the Northwest, a different atmosphere over Orcas Island . . . Rosario Yesterdays.

Christopher Peacock
Orcas Island

Robert Moran with "Keno"   (courtesy of Betty Moran Burns)

Rosario Yesterdays

I am now in my eighty-first year. I'm offering Rosario for sale to simplify the settlement of my estate when I am no longer here to give it my personal attention.

It is now over sixty-two years since I, a native of New York City, at the age of seventeen years, was, on a steerage ticket, dumped on Yesler Dock, Seattle, in November 1875.

At that date, Seattle was a sawmill town of about 1500 population. Yesler's Dock, at the foot of now Yesler Way was Seattle's only waterfront landing place. I got my breakfast that morning in a hash house at the head of the dock — on credit. That was easy to negotiate in those days . . .

It is too long a life story to detail here, except for me to say that I would like to travel again that sixty-two year old trail.

It's a history that would record an industrial self made life, from a breakfast on credit to the construction complete, in all its parts, of the first class battleship Nebraska; an industrial payroll that covered 22 acres of Seattle's waterfront.

Thirty-one years ago I left the shipbuilding business in Seattle. I was a nervous wreck. The doctors had me ticketed for Lake View Cemetery — due, as they said then, to organic heart disease. Doctors in those days were not as well informed as they are now on the ills of the human body.

My extreme nervous condition, due to mental overwork in a business way, misled the doctors to believe I had organic heart disease.

This period is now proved over a period of thirty-three years; now in my eighty-first year without a physical ailment. I had my physical examination, and doctors ultimatum 2 years before I actually retired.

The credit all goes to the industrious, though carefree life I have had in the exercise of my native construction inclination as a planner and builder of Rosario, creating that wonder scenic spot on this island, the Moran State Park. No architect or technical advisor can make any claim on what has been created by me on this island.

I believe I was born primarily a constructor. The rapid and intensive expansion of the shipbuilding business in Seattle gradually forced me from the constructive work I was born into. The executive position of office and management work was never to my liking.

Rosario, with my business worries gone, left me a free mind, to follow with my constructive work in evidence on Orcas Island. And now it is my desire—having in my mind uncertainties of life at my age—to simplify a settlement of my estate, while I am here, to do as I wish done.

If Rosario is sold the new owner will get from it what it gave me. In any event I have no plans that contemplate a residence, other than on this island, haven of rest and long life—a much more pleasant ending than falling from business desk, or conference table, into the undertaker's hands.

Robert Moran
A letter to the Seattle
Times. July 4, 1937.

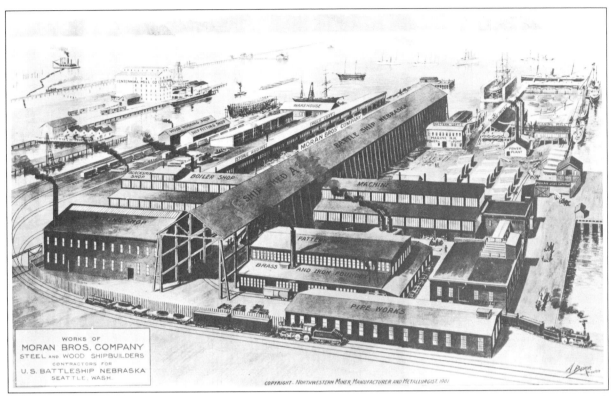

Drawing of Moran Bros. Plant, 1901. Drawing by A. Burr, Seattle.   (courtesy of Museum of History & Industry)

The Moran Mansion.   (courtesy of Rosario Resort)

Childhood Yesterdays

"Go West" Young Man

I was born January 26, 1857, at the East River end of Grand Street in New York City. The family tree record shows Irish-Dutch blood on the father's side and pure Scotch from the grandest mother of ten that ever lived.

Edward Moran, Robert Moran's father, was himself the son of an Irish stone mason and a machinist by trade. During the Civil War he was an engineer on a Northern warship, and one night, under cover of fire from Union forces, he crawled across the ice of the James River and spiked a gun on the opposite shore. The act made the young naval officer a hero; however, he returned from the service an embittered man, very hard to get along with.

Moving his family to Montclair, New Jersey, he contracted to make belts for Singer sewing machine, and put the boys to work on them. They rebelled early, most of them running away. Edward Jr., the eldest of the ten children, and Robert, the third boy, found apprenticeships as machinists in New York.

I was out of school and absolutely on my own resources at the age of fourteen year, and when I was seventeen I got the Horace Greeley "bug" in which he advised, as editor of the New York Tribune, that the young men "go west." I accepted his advice and started out on foot. My objective was San Francisco. I tramped as far as Cincinnati, where I secured employment in a scrap iron rolling mill on the banks of the Ohio River, as a millright's helper. I held that job during the summer, then returned to New York having decided to make my trip to San Francisco by the water route.

In September, 1875, Moran got together $150 and went to the Pacific Mail Steamship Company's office in New York, where he purchased a steerage ticket to San Francisco via the Panama route. This was about the time when the French had given up their effort to build a canal, but they left on the isthmus a narrow gauge railroad, which was used by the Pacific Mail Co. as a connecting link to its Atlantic and Pacific water services.

I arrived in San Francisco in October, 1875. I had no relative or friend on the coast, and as 1875 was a very depressed economic period, I could not secure employment in San Francisco, and, as my cash reserve ran low, I gave my last $15 to the Goodale-Perkins Steamship Company for a steerage ticket to Seattle. We were fed on "salt horse" and California red potatoes on the voyage up the coast, and I was dumped out without breakfast on Yesler's Wharf, the then only deep-water dock on the Seattle waterfront, at six o'clock in the morning, November 17, 1875.

As my capital account was then reduced to ten cents, I was in a very embarrassing social and economic condition. As I walked up the dock that morning before daylight, it was, as was natural that time of year, raining.

With the "luck of the Irish," Moran immediately picked up the wonderful aroma of a cooking breakfast, and found himself at Our House, a "hash house" at the foot of Yesler's Wharf. Moran met Big Bill Gross, the huge black proprietor of the restaurant, and explained to him that he had just arrived by steamer, and was without financial resources. But if his "face looked all right," he would like to negotiate credit, assuring Bill that he would pay him back as soon as he found employment. They struck a bargain, and Moran had a new economic start on life.

Bill was a fine cook and administered his own kitchen, with Mrs. Bill as dishwasher. Seattle had not then advanced in the culinary arts to a point where it seemed necessary to have short dressed, silk stockinged, permanent waved waitresses. The facts are that there was no available waiter material of female gender in those days. And none was needed, as far as Bill was concerned. He had cut a half-moon opening in the partition between the kitchen and dining room. Bill served in the kitchen, all on one plate, passed it through the half-moon, and called the patron to "come and get it." That breakfast was pork sausage and flapjacks with coffee. That

"You should have seen the one that got away!"
(courtesy of Rosario Resort)

Puget Sound fishing industry during late 1800's.
(courtesy of Rosario Resort)

*was the scent I had picked up on my
way up the dock that morning. Bill had
the window open and I presume that was
his method of advertising his bill of fare.*

Seattle was a small village of 1500 population,
named after a local Indian chief, Chief Sealth, and
Henry Yesler's saw mill was its heart. There was
a very depressed economy at the time throughout
the nation, but especially in those parts that were
trying to grow. The working day was twelve hours,
and ordinary laborer's compensation averaged
about two dollars. Men carried their blankets and
personal belongings on their backs from job to job
in logging camps and saw mills. The mattress was
provided by nature on the spot. Transportation
over Puget Sound country was by water, as roads
were few and mostly not passable by wagon
transportation.

*After filling up on Bill Gross' stable
fodder that morning, naturally my next
important problem was earning capacity.
My entire family was practically raised
and lived in a machine shop. Bill was
now financially interested in my earning*

*capacity, so directed me to the only
machine shop in Seattle at the time.
Visiting there, I found a young man
operating a lathe. He informed me that
he was the only machinist in town and
did not have work half the time. Up to
about a year ago, if you had visited my
son John's shop on First Avenue South,
the Moran Manufacturing Company, in
the back part of the shop, you would
have found an old man running a lathe.
That was the young man I talked with
sixty-four years ago. He had worked at
his trade as a machinist all his life.*

When Puget Sound logging camps needed a
cook, Bill Gross was the cook directory, and was
generally called on to supply such help. Moran's
board bill credit must have been getting to a
dangerous financial point in Bill's judgment, so he
asked young Moran if he had done any cooking.
Moran assured him that the culinary arts was one
of his various experiences, and convinced him that
he was particularly efficient at it.

After meeting Jim Brackett, the head of a logging
camp on Squak Slough, Moran was loaded with the

camp crew and supplies into a wagon. They followed a wagon trail between stumps over what today is Yesler Way, to Lake Washington, where the only power boat, the *James Mortie*, furnished transportation across the lake.

They transferred at the mouth of Squak Slough to the logger's boat, which took them up to the camp. The camp's dining, social, and sleeping activities were housed in a one–room log hut about twenty feet square, with three–high pyramided bunks and two small windows.

> *I was rather handicapped in demonstrating my culinary artistry by the fact that the standard camp food in those days was most plain, and varied only by consisting generally of sow belly pork, chili beans, flour, and potatoes with the green coffee beans from Guatemala, roasted by the cook, and sweetened by tar-like molasses.*
>
> *In those days, there was no store yeast. The cook, when he made a batch of bread, took a chunk of "germ dough" which he preserved in a small sack of dry flour. That was the personal "starter," and when he left the job he took the yeast germ with him. I found the Brackett Camp without yeast germ. Well, to make a long and disagreeable story short, after I had exercised my abilities for about three days, Brackett came to me and in a very confidential—but firm—way told me there seemed to be some dissatisfaction in the crew about the cooking, and that I better return to town. He said this in such a confidential way that he created in my mind the impression that the sooner I left the better, it might be physically for my future. He gave me three dollars, sent me down the Slough to what is now the University property in the company boat. The tramp from there, through virgin timber and windfalls, took me all day, and when I arrived in Seattle, my shoes were off my feet. Pinkham and Sax, the men's furnishing store, got Brackett's three dollars for a new pair.*

In a matter of days, the skipper of the steamer *J.B. Libby* put in an appearance at "Our House" in search of a deck hand. Bill Gross recommended Robert Moran and the career of the young man was initially launched.

The *J.B. Libby* was the only regular lifeline on the Sound, working the Seattle–Bellingham mail service of one mail a week. The voyage required two days from Seattle to the then "Seahome," the Bellingham Bay deep landing. The captain and crew were not only responsible for freight and mail, but stopped at settlements along the way to report the Sound's general news and gossip. Along the way the crew would deal with the local Indians to buy ducks, berries and other seasonal vegetables from their beach shanties, which dotted the shores of the Sound.

In those days, the boat landings were known as high water wharfs, high and dry at low tide. This required landing the passengers and freight with a small boat, and generally a long walk over the mud flats to reach dry land.

> *We reached Coupeville, on Whidbey Island, at extremely low tide, necessitating the small boat transfer. We had a Whidbey Island native daughter of one of the highly respected pioneer families as a passenger to be landed at Coupeville. This necessitated a "pig-a-back" transfer of the young lady over the mud flats to land, by one of the crew. I was drafted for the job of transporting the young lady, for the reason that I was the only member of the crew who had a pair of gum boots. Why the fireman needed a pair of gum boots in the boiler room was a mystery, as, while the old "Libby" was leaky, she never quite leaked badly enough that a fireman needed rubber boots in the boiler room.*
>
> *However, I was elected to make the "pig-a-back" transfer, and so far as I ever heard, did a satisfactory job. The native daughter afterward married one of our most respected and loved members. A few years ago, they visited at Rosario. During the dinner conversation, I mentioned the above transfer incident. The lady remembered the details, but had no recollection of the personality of the motive power that made the transfer over the tide flats. I modestly allowed the conversation to change.*

Moran moved from steamer to steamer during his first year in Seattle. One day at Yesler's pier, he was topping off his watertanks on the steamer *Zephyr,* when Captain George W. Bulline, a Federal boiler inspector, stepped up and introduced himself. In the future, Robert would meet presidents, congressmen and leaders of industry, but none would make as critical an impression on his future as this man. Bulline sensed something special in

Robert, and it was he, over the next few years, that would help broaden the good young machinist's knowledge to include mathematics, drafting and engineering, preparing him for his life's work.

The two men went to work directly. There was a fee involved for Bulline's services, but that included use of his library, periodic testing and endless consultation. Robert built a small water tight trunk to carry books and papers, safely protected from bilge water, steam and rain. Spare minutes were not spent on idle chatter with ship's crew and passengers. They were now spent on the books.

Moran pursued his studies and planned his future, quickly advancing in rank from deckhand at $25 a month to fireman at $40. He gained valuable experience, making friends and building a strong reputation that would stand for years to come.

In the territorial days of 1876, the courts were administered by district judges, appointed by the President. Court was held at various points where needed. This meant that the entire court contingent traveled by water to the various important settlements in the Puget Sound District, for there were no passage roads. Justice was usually administered in a direct and simple method.

I was at the time fireman on a stern wheeler steamer then in the Seattle-Snohomish service. United States District Court was to be opened for business in the town of Snohomish, located on the Snohomish River, then in the late seventies the principal settlement in what is now Snohomish County, a period before Everett was even thought of, not a single habitation where the city is now located. On the beach that is now Everett's waterfront, docks and mills, there was one lonely shack in which the caretaker of the telegraph line, where it crosses the Snohomish River, kept his tools and equipment. It was practically an all-day ride from Seattle to Snohomish. I have remembrance of one notable instance which showed in detail how justice was passed out in Territorial days.

We took the entire court organization, Judge and lawyers, aboard at Seattle for Snohomish. To break the monotony of the all day voyage, the favorite time-killer was a game of poker. On that trip, it developed that our District Judge was not an expert poker player. He was resourceful in the administration of justice. On this referred to voyage, with the court and lawyers there was an old time boss

logger, who had an important case of his own to come before the court at Snohomish. Our Judge had previously boasted that he was no novice at the game of poker. The logger took a hand with the Judge, and at the end of the game, the logger had $10 of the Judge's money.

When court convened the next morning in Snohomish Town Hall, the logger's case was the first on the docket. During the trial, the logger, who acted as his own attorney, took exception to a ruling the Judge made in the logger's case. The logger rose and in a loud voice informed the Judge that he "could not do that." Whereupon, the Judge ordered him to sit down, and informed him that he was fined $10 for contempt of court, which of course meant that the Judge had recovered the $10 lost the day before in the poker game.

A notable appointment by the President as District Judge was an outstanding Christian gentleman, Roger S. Green, learned in the law, a dispenser of exact justice, without fear or favor. Court was held in a room over a grocery store on Front Street, now First Avenue, in Seattle. The Judge was not provided with a raised dias; he sat with the lawyers and attendants on the floor level. Judge Green was inclined to be near-sighted.

In the trial of a case, counsel present included Thomas Burke, who was rather short of stature. There was also in the case an old time lawyer from Olympia, Judge McFadden. He stood, as I remember, nearly seven feet high. He and Burke were seated together before the Court; Burke standing was not as tall as McFadden when sitting, so when Judge Burke arose and started to address the Court, Judge Green directed him to stand up when addressing the Court. To which Burke replied that, if it please his Honor he was standing, whereupon Judge Green commanded Judge McFadden to sit down. To which McFadden informed Judge Green that if it pleased his Honor, he was sitting down.

In another case before Judge Green, one of the attorneys made reference to a former decision in a similar case of Greene versus Blank. In calling the Court's attention, he emphasized the name Greene with an "e" on its end. Judge Green took exception to the "e," and asked the lawyer if he would include the "e" in pronouncing his, the Judge's name. To which the lawyer replied, "That, your Honor, would depend altogether on how you decide this case!"

Alaska Days with John Muir

Captain Nat H. Lane, Jr. got in touch with Robert through Bill Gross in 1879. The captain was taking command of the new steamer *Cassiar,* and wanted Moran as his chief engineer for the steamer's Stikeen River Alaska trade.

When the season on the Stikeen closed, the vessel came to Victoria, put under British flag, and entered the Fraser River trade from New Westminster to Yale, the head of navigation. In that service, we transported to Yale the steel rails for the construction of the Canadian Pacific Railroad. That, of course, was before the terminus of the Canadian Pacific had been fixed at what is now the City of Vancouver. Then there was no settlement at what is Vancouver, on Burrards Inlet, a small saw mill and bunk house only.

During his three years with the *Cassiar,* Moran was fortunate to become friends with John Muir, the world renowned naturalist. The two men first met when Muir was a guest of the regional Presbyterian mission that chartered the *Cassiar* to visit their outpost settlements of Chilcat and Thlinket tribes to "ascertain their spiritual needs."

Robert Moran became fascinated by Muir's approach to nature and spirituality, and learned from his tales of adventure throughout the West. In return, Muir got first hand information on regional mining and lumbering practices from the young engineer.

On this trip the group inspected several deserted native villages. Muir was astounded by the sophisticated construction still evident in the partially standing ruins. He made sketches for Moran, who elected to remain with his ship at all times.

The *Cassiar* had experienced boiler troubles, and Moran was kept busy making temporary repairs. He explained to Muir the trouble was due to the steamer's movement between saltwater and fresh water, and explained to him the intricacies of the cooling system. Muir suspected some of the trouble was planned by his new friend, the engineer.

Moran was given a better offer as engineer on the *Gertrude,* traveling the Fraser River of British Columbia, where he crossed paths with Muir again. The two spent many more hours together, and Robert offered Muir overalls and a shovel full-time.

In Moran's travels to the various villages, he kept a mental inventory of where good tools and machinery were located, and assisted others with his knowledge of machine work. He learned from other seamen of the eccentricities of Alaska's Japanese current and weather, which would be of great benefit in a few years.

Frank, Robert, William and Sherman Moran.   (courtesy of Rosario Resort)

Seattle Yesterdays

Aware of Robert's success in the Northwest, older brothers Edward and Peter soon arrived in Seattle. In November of 1881 Robert married Melissa Paul, and the entire family lived together on Denny Hill. Melissa was born 4 days before her husband in London, Ontario, and came to Seattle by way of Victoria. When Robert met her she worked as a domestic in a close friend's home, and after courting her in the traditional fashion, he won her—much to his surprise.

Moran had also saved $500 to furnish transportation for his mother, five younger brothers and two sisters from New York to Seattle, something he had planned since his arrival in Seattle seven years earlier.

Prior and for many years, Wells Fargo operated on the coast and across the continent, not only an express business, but also it did much of the banking business, making it possible for coast merchants to purchase Wells Fargo drafts on its New York branch for the payment of bills. It was in that way that I forwarded the money for payment of transportation of Mother, sisters and brothers to Seattle. Wells Fargo's agent gave me the triplicate drafts, all the same on their faces, excepting that one of the drafts had a very large figure one on its face, another had a large figure two on its face, and the third had a large figure three on its face. On the figure "One" draft, there was printed, "This draft is good, Number 2 and 3 being unpaid." The figure "Two" draft had printed on it, "This draft is good, Numbers 1 and 3 being unpaid," and there was printed on Figure "Three" draft, "This draft is good, Numbers 1 and 2 being unpaid."

Now the purpose of issuing the three triplicate drafts was that prior to the period of which I write, the mail was carried across the continent by "Pony Express." Much of that mail was overhauled and destroyed by the Indians,

Robert Moran in his office at the Moran Bros. Co.

(courtesy of Whatcom County Museum)

which of course delayed delivery of coast merchants' drafts to eastern territory. With the triplicate drafts, you were directed to put one in today's mail for your eastern correspondent. In the following mail, you put No. 2, and again in another mail, you sent No. 3 draft, all for payment of the same eastern account. This system assured if the Indians got No. 1 or No. 2 drafts, the eastern merchant would get No. 3. At the time of which I write, the Union Pacific Railroad had been completed across the continent, which insured a more safe mail, though Wells Fargo continued the above triplicate system for some time after.

This, of course, was all before there were sleeping cars for immigrant tickets. They got what sleep they could sitting up as best they could. When they arrived in San Francisco, they came to Portland by steamer, thence via the then Northern Pacific Railroad from Kalama to Tacoma, and by the stern wheel steamer, "Emma Hayward" Tacoma to Seattle. When they arrived I had a house and primitive furnishings ready for them in Seattle.

When his family arrived, Moran quit steamboat engineering at the age of 25, and with a capital of $1600 started a marine repair shop on Yesler Wharf with his brothers. Robert, having spotted the necessary tools and machinery up and down the Sound, set out with his brothers to acquire the needed equipment.

Robert was hired as vice-president and general manager of the Seattle Drydock and Shipbuilding Company by Bailey Gatzert, president of the company—a very successful businessman and considered one of Seattle's "fathers." Through Gatzert, Moran was able to acquire the property next to the Shipbuilding Company for his own machine shop.

In 1883 the business bought the 80 ton stern wheeler *Josephine*, which had been seriously damaged when its boiler exploded and killed eight people. The new shop worked night and day refurbishing the steamer and had it resold and back in business in record time. The overhaul of the *Josephine* began a great shipbuilding saga in Northwest history.

Mayor Moran

The brothers prospered, and in 1887 Robert Moran was elected to the City Council. Seattle had grown to a population of 20,000 and Moran was well-respected among his fellow businessmen and the city "fathers."

In 1888, Fredrick Grant of the Post-Intelligencer newspaper called a few of the office boys together and asked them to prepare lists of working men who might be able to win the Mayor's office from the Populists. In the previous election, a populist candidate beat the venerable Arthur A. Denny, incumbent mayor and Seattle's founding father. Grant, as well as the city's "fathers," wanted a Republican nominee for the convention. When the lists were submitted, the name Robert Moran came up first and no other names were considered.

Mr. Grant called upon Robert and found him in overalls in his machine shop, hands covered with grease. At first Moran thought it all a joke, but agreed to think it over a few days. Later he said he would agree if the nomination came to him without solicitation or effort on his part. It came that way and he was elected overwhelmingly. At 31 years of age, Moran thought this would be a nice challenge for his career, and he accepted the office.

Indeed it was a challenge, for the following year Seattle was destroyed by the great fire of June 6, 1889.

Seattle Fire

The fire started when workers in a cabinet shop were heating glue on a gas stove and allowed it to overheat. The glue boiled over and ignited turpentine soaked woodshavings on the floor. Flames quickly engulfed the basement shop on First Street (1st Ave.) near Madison St.

The city's two fire engines soon arrived, and the first went to pump saltwater—but the tide was out and hoses could not reach the water. The other engine began to hook hoses up on the water mains, but pressure quickly fell, and within minutes the streams were so weak they wouldn't reach the top of the building.

Within twenty minutes fire had spread through the entire block. Mayor Moran took command from a distressed James Murphy, the acting fire chief (the regular fire chief was in San Francisco attending a convention on fire fighting methods), and ordered the Coleman block blown up to form a fire gap. With a cheer from the gathered crowd, the Palace Restaurant was leveled with a large charge of dynamite. Unfortunately, the fire swept quickly over the wreckage and spread to the wharfs.

In minutes Yesler Wharf and the Moran Bros. repair shop was the heart of the fire, and when it was over, thirty blocks covering more than sixty acres were destroyed.

Beginning of Seattle Fire — June 6, 1889.   (courtesy of Museum of History & Industry)

Mayor Moran presided at the meeting of citizens held the next morning, and his enthusiastic support of the measure there adopted had great influence in restoring confidence among the people. He favored rebuilding and remodeling the streets, restrictions as to building in the fire district, and other measures which were finally carried out and which made the present Seattle such an improvement on the old.

All this caused by an inadequate water system, an issue that was not new to Mayor Moran.

> *My most notable work as Mayor was the conclusion of negotiations to close down the then Spring Hill Water Co.'s contaminated Lake Washington water supply, by purchase of its inadequate plant that was largely responsible, by its primitive water supply, that the city was destroyed by fire in 1889.*

Before the fire, Mayor Moran was fighting bitterly for public-ownership of the water system in Seattle. So, too, were the Populists, from whom he had won the office. This created a problem, not only because he was in favor of the Populists, but also because the water system was owned, among others, by his boss—Bailey Gatzert. The city ''fathers'' convinced Moran that Seattle would not be able to afford public-ownership (the private owners were making a net profit of $91,000 a year), and politician Moran wisely let the issue die . . . until June 6, 1889, the day Seattle burned.

In the post fire election on July 8, the public-ownership question was presented to voters and won by 97%. Moran was reelected as mayor and hired the eminent hydraulic engineer, Benezette Williams of Chicago (who had planned that city's sewage system), to begin work on Seattle's water, power and sewage system.

In all, the fire turned out to be a blessing for Seattle, creating opportunity for planned growth and development—a chance to become a real city.

Mayor Moran called on the National Guard to keep order.
(courtesy of the Museum of History & Industry)

Seattle became a "tent city" after the fire.
(courtesy of the Museum of History & Industry)

The outlook for opportunity in Seattle was so great that the population nearly doubled within six months! Moran was responsible not only for the strong leadership during Seattle's rebuilding, but also for the city's municipally-owned water system.

Moran Brothers Company

The Moran brothers had built their firm from a capital of $1600 to a factory worth over $40,000 when the big fire swept it away. Fortunately, just before this time—and due to their rapid growth—the firm had secured a tract of tide land at the foot of Charles Street, and had completed preliminary arrangements for moving to that location.

They quickly constructed temporary buildings on this land, and a new shop was open and ready for business on June 16, just ten days after the old plant's destruction. Through the rebuilding of Seattle, increased demands were made upon the new plant, necessitating the employment of more capital in the business. The result was formation of the Moran Brothers Company, with a capital stock of $250,000 on December 19, 1889. Robert Moran was President, Secretary and Treasurer, Peter Moran was Vice-President, Sherman Moran was Assistant Superintendent in charge of wood working, Frank Moran was Foundry Foreman and Edward Moran was an executive without title.

When the fire swept away the machine shop it also destroyed a complete stock of machinists' and engineers' supplies the company had been selling. Shortly after moving to Charles St., the Moran Bros. Co. opened a salesroom at the old location, under the name Moran Brothers and Durie. The latter dropped out of the firm a few years later and it became the Moran Supply Company, which enjoyed a large patronage.

Nationally speaking, 1893 was a slow year, but the Moran Bros. Co. prospered. By now the yard covered 26 acres and was equipped with a large marine railway that could haul any sound steamer out of the water in 12 minutes. Whenever a ship was disabled and in need of repair somewhere in the North Pacific, Lloyd's of London usually advised the skipper to put in at the Moran Shipyard. They had built an international reputation for honest, efficient shipbuilding and repair.

Perhaps the best evidence of rapid growth was their first United States Government job in 1895. Moran Bros. had contracted to furnish the steam plant of the U.S. dry dock at Charleston Navy Yard with boilers, engines and pumps. All machinery was manufactured in Seattle, and the pumps—designed by Robert Moran—could deliver one million gallons of water every five minutes! This

Moran residence on Capitol Hill, Seattle — 1898.
(courtesy of Rosario Resort)

The Moran Bros. Co. meetings often took place on Sundays after church at the shipyards, with the entire family making an outing of it. A close family corporation, not a dollar of outside capital was invested nor a share of stock sold outside the family. (courtesy of the Whatcom County Museum)

equipment was installed at the Charleston Navy Yard, but government inspectors refused to accept the pumps, claiming they were not according to specifications. Moran shipped a pump to Washington, D.C., and demonstrated his design capability. He obtained a decision which not only overruled the inspectors but pronounced his pumps the best in existence.

Moran began to make the rounds of naval offices in Washington, D.C. His eager, honest, straightforward manner was new to the bureaucrats, who had been dealing with the same east coast shipbuilders for so long that everything was taken for granted.

On subsequent trips east the Moran Bros. Co. President made quiet side trips to major yards where he took notes on procedures. He was surprised to find himself a welcome curiosity to the eastern moguls, many of whom had never been west of the Mississippi.

Moran also felt at ease with Senator Watson Squire, who seldom was visited by his constituents in the nation's capital. Squire was Governor of Washington Territory and became Senator at State-

hood in 1889. On trips up and down the west coast he was amazed to find that only San Francisco had any type of defense. He convinced his colleagues that Puget Sound was actually one of the finest harbors in the country. Squire went after federal money for defense installations on Puget Sound, including lighthouses, revenue and customs patrols, making the Moran Bros. Co. a busy place.

With the influence of Senator Squire, and a successful bid by the Moran Bros., an announcement was made in the fall of 1895 that a U.S. Navy torpedo boat would be built in Seattle. The Morans had won the contract over Zwicker Iron Works of Portland and the Union Iron Works of San Francisco with the lowest bid. It was obvious to the navy that the company would not make any money out of the contract, and the firm did not expect to. However, it was an opportunity to show that a torpedo boat could be built in Seattle, bringing hope for the future of Northwest shipbuilding.

The brothers were jubilant when William Moran came in with another successful bid at almost the same time. He had stolen the contract for the Coast Guard boarding boat *Golden Gate* right out from

Moran Brothers Co. docks on Elliott Bay.
(courtesy of Rosario Resort)

View of Seattle waterfront from Moran Bros. Co.
(courtesy of Rosario Resort)

under the noses of all Pacific Coast builders. The *Golden Gate* keel blocks were placed beside the torpedo boat and she would be the first all-steel boat built and launched in Washington State.

The yard was bursting with "bread and butter" building projects and there was always an audience watching the two boats take shape. The Moran Bros. had not only anticipated the shift to metal fabrication, but Robert had also acquired L.H. McMurtie from the Maryland Steel Company as chief of new construction.

The days when the Moran Bros. made all decisions in the family business were over. Government contracts called for in-plant inspectors. Robert had noted the rather fancy offices in the nation's capital in which navy officers enjoyed shades of class and tradition, so he added two beautifully furnished offices at his plant for the inspectors. A fine, friendly view of the harbor and waterfront activity was offered—in hopes that inspectors would stay put and out of the hair of the working men.

Actually, Moran found the inspectors enjoyable to have around, receiving compliments from them often. Lt. Spear, inspector of the torpedo boat, had nothing but praise for the Moran operation:

> *"I am much pleased with him personally and officially. I am impressed with his business-like energy and vim. Why, I had not been in the office five minutes when he shot a question at me about the lines of the boat that made me put on my thinking cap, and showed me at once his intelligence and his pride and interest in his work. He differs essentially from the ordinary contractors with whom I've dealt. They are usually listless and indifferent to all save the mere fulfillment of the letter of the contract. Moran evidently feels personal*

> *pride in his work with a rare fore-sight..."*

Another inspector in the plant was W.W. Bush, an experienced engineer who had been over the waves from coast to coast. A very good natured fellow who was not new to Seattle, Bush enjoyed telling this story at the shipyards:

> *"It was just after the big fire and Seattle was a stinking pile of ashes and tents. I'd had a pay day and at least one pocket was full. I found a place to buy a bottle and another shack with some games going, but the ladies were somewhere's else. The fun shops had burned right along with the churches and court house. I paid a dollar for a pile of hay and a blanket, in a tent. And, stayed awake all night, sipping on my jug, afraid to go to sleep so no one could rob me. Bob Moran was mayor then and running around giving orders and telling everyone Seattle would rise again. And now, just a few years later, here we are in the same spot, with fine buildings and everyone getting along, like Bob said they would, only this time I'm giving the orders and Moran will have to do the listening."*

An impressive list of Seattle's top names, along with 4,000 citizens, were present for the launching of Revenue tug *Golden Gate* in February, 1897. Moran knew the tide wouldn't he high enough at the scheduled noon launch, so the night before he had a dredger take out 3 feet of bottom. Everything went perfectly, the ship was outfitted, accomplished more than the required 13 knots and was moved to San Francisco Bay.

In October of that year the Morans received a telegram notifying them that in an informal race with the ferry *San Rafael*, the *Golden Gate* had become the fastest boat on San Francisco Bay. Further, not a drop had been spilled from a glass of water placed over the propeller. This information, with "best regards," was from the captain of the boat.

When the torpedo boat (officially named the *Rowan*) was launched the following year, 10,000 people gathered for the event. The government had called for a speed of 26 knots, and would not accept the ship if it attained less than 25. The *Rowan* was clocked at 28.97 knots on its trial run, nearly doubling the speed of boats in service.

Gold!

During the summer and fall of 1897, every boat arriving from the North brought news of gold discoveries in Alaska. This meant a boon for Seattle, as the Yukon bound were outfitted and supplied in the city. Moran Bros. Co., swamped with business, lost many of their key personnel in the rush north. Most employees came to the office and made some attempt to explain why they were leaving steady work, in pleasant surroundings, to seek their fortunes in the "ice box of the world." They all had an exciting dream, many feeling sorry for the brothers not being able to join the merry stampede.

But the brothers struck gold themselves in the rush north, refitting old boats and supplying them with new machinery, as well as thawing machines, drills for working frozen ground, and many other tools and machines in demand. The company advertised in Eastern papers for workers to replace those lost: "Requesting ships' carpenters, plankers, caulkers and first class mechanics, wages

The Alaskan gold rush created many projects for the Moran Bros. Co., including these river steamers for the Yukon River trade.
(courtesy of the Whatcom County Museum)

35¢ per hour. We have no time to carry on correspondence." The work force at the yard went from 350 to a peak of over 2,000 men working day and night.

"Gold discovered in the Klondike" was a universal headline, and adventurers from all parts of the world began their quest in Seattle. Since ocean and Yukon River transportation from Seattle was very limited in those days, the common method for gold hunters to reach pay dirt was overland from Skagway, by trail to the upper waters of the Yukon, then down river by canoe to Dawson, the headquarters. The quantity of winter supplies that could be backpacked from Skagway to Dawson was extremely limited.

This winter food supply for the thousands presented a serious problem to avoid great winter suffering, if not starvation. This was a problem that was immediately taken in hand by Seattle's merchants and civic leaders. Ocean service from Seattle to St. Michael was not a serious problem; ample ships were available. The thousand miles of river transportation was not so easily disposed of. Moran Brothers Company worked out a plan that accomplished the river service by constructing on Seattle's tide lands near where the Union Depot now stands, fourteen stern wheel river steamers, each 175 feet long, 35 feet beam, and in addition 4 river freight barges. All of these 18 vessels, including engines and boilers, were complete, ready for the coast voyage to St. Michael within six months, there being on the company's payroll at the time over twenty-one hundred men.

Two of the above steamers were set up in frame in Seattle, then knocked down and shipped by ocean route to Dutch Harbor in the Aleutian Islands, together with their engines, boilers and other material, with a gang of mechanics, where they completed the two vessels during the winter and gave early summer food relief service on the river from St. Michael.

The balance of the fleet of sixteen vessels made the Alaska coast voyage under their own power, giving delivery in St. Michael early enough for all the steamers to make one—and some two—voyages up the Yukon before ice closed the river for the winter, thus relieving what might have been, without this river service, a very serious food condition on the upper Yukon that following winter.

The delivery at St. Michael of this fleet of eighteen vessels was no ordinary marine problem. So far as I know, a similar sea voyage of that number of shallow draft river service vessels had never been attempted. There was first the hazard of the sea on a long, dangerous coast line. Second, there was the problem of fuel supply and fresh water for the boilers, and lastly, the selection of crews from thousands of adventurers whose only thought was to reach the source of gold at the earliest moment. In the selection of the crew came first the choice of the best Alaska coast pilot, and next the various captains, none of whom could have had previous experience in such an Alaska coast voyage.

When the twelve Yukon river steamers were launched and completed for the ocean voyage to St. Michael, the first problem to solve was fuel for the trip. This was solved by sending an inspector out over the Sound country to locate dry cord wood, as 1,500 cords of four-foot wood would be needed. After this wood was located at various points, the steamers were sent to gather it. The lower holds of the vessels were jammed solid full of this dry cord wood, which acted as a life preserver. The vessel could not sink after taking on wood fuel. The captains had orders to proceed to Roche Harbor on San Juan Island, and await further orders. Roche Harbor was selected as the initial starting point for the voyage by the inside passage up the Alaskan coast, as it was the most northerly customs house from which we secured our clearance papers.

The services of a coast pilot named Edward Lennan were secured. He had the reputation of being the best informed Alaska and British Columbia pilot. Three ocean tugs were chartered to accompany the fleet of sixteen vessels and render aid if needed. The crews of all told consisted of about 200 men, who were signed up for the voyage by the United States Shipping Commission. Food stores of over ten tons were supplied, and when the entire fleet had arrived at Roche Harbor, the writer of this, along with the pilot, clerk, and

The Moran built Yukon River Fleet at Roche Harbor, San Juan Island — 1898.
(courtesy of the Whatcom County Museum)

stenographer, took passage on one of the steamers for Roche Harbor, from which point the customs were cleared for the entire fleet, now with the three ocean tug convoy, consisted of nineteen vessels, and steamed away for the Comax Coal Mines of British Columbia, where each vessel of the fleet took thirty tons of coal on deck. Note: these vessels had all been prepared for heavy weather on the coast by building "whale-backs" over the entire bows of the vessels; also, they were all built for fresh water service; that is, with high pressure, non-condensing engines. Surface condensers with circulating pumps had to be fitted temporarily for the ocean voyage, so as to guard against salt water getting into the boilers.

After coaling at Comax, we sailed away up the inside passage. The voyage up the coast was uneventful until we passed out into the Pacific, where the rolling sea swell made it rather uncomfortable. However, we reached Yakutat, a fine harbor close up to Cook's Inlet. It was my plan to lay by at Yakutat for three days to give the engineers and crews time to overhaul and prepare for the extended voyage where the waters would not be so peaceful as they had been in the inside passage.

The next morning after arriving at Yakutat, at about nine o'clock, a small boat came alongside the "Pilgrim," my vessel, the boatman passing to the writer a large sealed legal looking envelope. Upon opening it, I found it to be a "sea-lawyer" protest, formulated by the captains of two of the river boats. In substance, they protested against proceeding any further on the voyage, giving as their reasons that a continuation would be dangerous to life and property. That was mutiny, as we understand such action by a vessel's crew. You can imagine the position they were attempting to put me in, with over half a million dollars worth of property, contracted to be delivered at St. Michael within a specified time freight service to relieve thousands with a food supply at the upper reaches of the Yukon River.

This protest created a situation that required prompt action by me. I was satisfied that the balance of the crews on the vessels had no knowledge of this two-captain document, so before the poison became epidemic, a radical cure was necessary. When the entire fleet came to anchor the night before, as stated above, it was the intention to remain at Yakutat Harbor two or three days for refitting before proceeding on the voyage. Immediately upon receiving that protest, at nine o'clock the next morning, I ordered my clerk to take a small boat and notify all the captains of the entire fleet, other than the two protesting captains, to have steam up and prepare to leave the harbor within two hours. In the meantime, I took a boat and removed the two protesting captains from their vessels and landed them on the beach, where they had a safe harbor against their fears of ship wreck. This gave them a rest-up for nearly thirty days before the mail boat returned them to Seattle.

After safely landing the two captains, I returned to the fleet, promoted mates to captains, deckhands to mates, and the entire fleet left Yakutat Harbor at eleven o'clock. I afterward found out that the balance of crew had no knowledge of the two captains' action. It was a prompt cure which, if not taken energetically in hand, would probably have been developed in a more serious way by those two "cold-feet" captains later in the voyage, where we experienced more troublesome waters down in the Aleutian Islands to Dutch Harbor.

We then proceeded up the coast. When off the mouth of Cook's Inlet, we met one of the fierce "wooleys" that blow out of Cook's Inlet and for which those waters are noted. We struggled on into Katmai

Straits with a continuing of the Cook's Inlet storm. We got no shelter and our convoy tugs came into good use in chasing blown-away boats and returning them to their anchorages off the mouth of the Katmai River. However, as the storm continued, our three tugs could not recover the river boats as fast as they were driven seaward, and one of them went on the rocks and was a total loss as a Yukon River transport. However, she finally served a good purpose, as the members of the Indian mission at Katmai recovered all the material of the wreck and used it to build a church.

Note here that my company sustained no financial loss from the wreck, as before the fleet left Seattle, it was insured for safe delivery at St. Michael by Lloyd's of London for close to a half million dollars and at premium cost of over twenty-four thousand dollars. I can say in connection with this insurance loss, that when Lloyd's received word that the Moran fleet had arrived safely in St. Michael with the loss of only one of sixteen vessels, they were much pleased and made prompt payment of the loss.

On to Dutch Harbor was an uneventful part of the trip, except we were compelled to take shelter from the sea at a number of points down by the Aleutian Islands. From Dutch Harbor, we followed the east shallow shore of Bering Sea past the mouth of the Kuskikwin and Yukon Rivers to St. Michael.

Some of the steamers were short of fuel

T. C. Power built by Moran Bros. at Dutch Harbor for Yukon River. Winter of 1898.
(courtesy of the Museum of History & Industry)

Moran Brothers Company Drydock. Built in 1900 it was 400 ft. long, 60 ft. between towers, with 8,000 tons displacement.
(courtesy of Rosario Resort)

when we arrived at Dutch Harbor. This was replenished with coal that we dug out of the side of the shore line of Bristol Bay at the entrance to Bering Sea. The coal was exposed and all we had to do was pry it out of the side of the cliff with steel bars.

There was no sickness or other accidents on the voyage of forty days, other than those recorded here.

The Morans were confronted with a problem in building these boats: in order to service the Yukon River effectively they had to be of light draft; however, they also had to be of sufficient strength to withstand the 4,000 mile journey from Seattle to St. Michael. Not only was successful design and construction a triumph for the steamboat builders, but the journey from Seattle to St. Michael under Robert Moran's command remains a most astonishing navigational feat.

The personal family triumph was overshadowed by the death of younger brother Paul Moran. He was in charge of reassembling a steamer that had been knocked down in Seattle and shipped earlier to Alaska, where he died of diabetes. Robert adopted Paul's daughter Mary and raised her along with his own four children.

U.S.S. Nebraska

By 1900 the Moran Brothers Company had grown to such proportions that a large dry dock was built. This was in addition to the marine railway for hauling out smaller boats, and a huge saw

and planning mill that was in operation. The mill was capable of producing timber 48 inches square and 125 ft. long, turning out 100,000 board feet daily.

By the fall of 1900, the Secretary of the Navy called for bids on a number of big battleships authorized by Congress the year before—at the end of the Spanish-American war.

When the writer appeared at the Navy Department in Washington with a proposal to build in "that sawmill town of Seattle" what was in those days a first class battleship, some of the Department organization probably had no knowledge of such a place as Seattle, so it appeared quite a joke to some of the Navy organization that a firm that had never built a battleship should presume to enter competition against the older established naval builders.

The facts were that the so-called old naval constructors were no better informed on naval construction than was Moran Bros. Company. At any rate, the law required that contracts be awarded to the lowest bidders, and as my company was prepared to furnish the bond, we were on an equal footing with the so-called older shipyards.

Congress had authorized the construction of four of the "Nebraska" class ships and made a definite cost appropriation for the completion of the vessels. This bound the Navy constructors

During 1901, the brothers began to expand their shipyard in preparation for the building of the USS NEBRASKA. This structure housed the battleship.
(courtesy of Rosario Resort)

to design ships the total cost of which would not exceed the sum authorized by Congress. The Navy Department, in its desire to get the most ship for the money available, expanded its plans to a point where, when the bids were open in Washington, all were found to be approximately three hundred thousand dollars in excess of the sum appropriated by Congress. The bidders were then told by the Secretary of the Navy that all bids would be rejected unless they were scaled down to the amount of money cost available.

In the case of my company's bid, it was required to be reduced about three hundred fifty thousand dollars. Of the above sum, the Navy organization cut about fifty thousand dollars cost from the specifications, which in my company's case left about three hundred thousand dollars to be cut from our bid. The writer was in Washington at the time. I fully realized how important it was that Seattle secure a contract for one of these ships, so concluded to advise the Seattle Chamber of Commerce of the facts by wire. In this, I advised that if the Chamber would undertake to secure subscriptions from Seattle businessmen and citizens for the sum of one hundred thousand dollars, my company would contribute two hundred thousand, making the three hundred thousand reduction on our bid, which would secure the award of the contract. The Seattle Chamber of Commerce acted promptly on this,

secured the full hundred thousand pledge to be paid only when the ship was launched in Seattle.

A small group of businessmen started by pledging $32,900. Within three days 536 citizens had pledged the entire $100,000, and more. The Moran Brothers Company won the contract.

Seattle held a big celebration when the keel of the *U.S.S. Nebraska (BB14)* was laid on July 4, 1902. Bands played and a large crowd cheered when the first red hot rivets were driven in the great plates of steel by Gov. Henry McBride of Washington and Gov. Ezra P. Savage of Nebraska.

For more than two years the Moran Bros. Co. was the scene of immense activity. More than 1,000 additional workmen were employed and about two million was paid out in wages on account of the battleship. The building of the *Nebraska* had become a Seattle institution.

The Moran girls.
(courtesy of the Whatcom County Museum)

Sherman, Frank and William Moran with Company Foreman Harry Fox — 1904.   (courtesy of Rosario Resort)

Moran family gathering at the shipyards.   (courtesy of Rosario Resort)

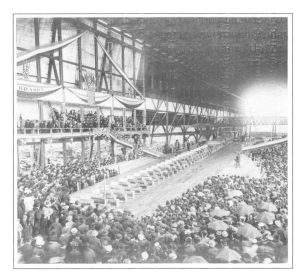

Introducing Governor Savage at the commencement of ceremonies, Moran Bros. Co., July 4, 1902.
(courtesy of Rosario Resort)

Governor Savage of the State of Nebraska, speaking at the laying of the keel ceremony.
(courtesy of Betty Moran Burns)

Laying of the keel, U.S.S. Nebraska. Driving the first rivet.
(courtesy of Rosario Resort)

NEBRASKA's hull begins to take shape.
(courtesy of Rosario Resort)

When launching day came on October 7, 1904, Robert Moran had reached the apex of his shipbuilding career. The honors he had won as mayor in the late 1880's were overshadowed. He was the outstanding figure of the celebration Seattle staged, though the Governors of two states and many other dignitaries were present.

One of the largest crowds ever assembled in Seattle up to that time saw the *Nebraska* hit the water. Some 40,000 people crowded the Moran Shipyards and adjoining waterfront, with another 15,000 in boats on Elliot Bay. Gov. John H. Mickey of Nebraska made the big oration of the day when he spoke for the people of Nebraska, accepting the honor done their state. Robert Moran in the meantime was directing a crew of workmen who were chopping away the keel blocks. He was more interested in a successful launching than the speeches. He wanted to make sure the ship went down the ways while the tide was right at 2:13 p.m.

But eleven minutes ahead of schedule, while Seattle district Congressman William E. Humphrey was putting his finishing touches on the last of the speeches, the *Nebraska* began to move. In the excitement of knocking out the holding blocks, the crew let the ship get away and she started sliding at 2:02 p.m. Miss Mary Nain Mickey, the ship's sponsor and daughter of the Governor of Nebraska, realized what was happening and without a moment of hesitation cracked the champagne bottle squarely on the battleship's bow and let out the traditional christening words. The crowd began cheering, warships lining the Sound boomed salutes, and brass bands struck up the "Nebraska March," a piece written especially for the occasion.

The *Nebraska* moved down the ways which smoked under the friction and weight, and a moment later was plowing through the water heading for the West Seattle shore. Tugs caught her and it was the beginning of many celebrations that night in Seattle.

As part of the launching ceremony, John Schram, then president of the Seattle Chamber of Commerce, turned over to a representative of the Moran Bros. Co. a certified check for $100,000, making good the city's pledge to see Robert Moran through.

Planned at a time when the Navy was adopting new ideas regarding construction, the *Nebraska* spent the next two years at the shipyards under-

Workmen inspect interior of NEBRASKA's all-steel hull.
(courtesy of Rosario Resort)

Preparation for launching — 1904.
(courtesy of Rosario Resort)

Workmen stand proud before launching.
(courtesy of Rosario Resort)

going more changes than any other ship in the Navy at the time. With each successive bureau change in Washington, changes were ordered in the ship, all of which consumed a great deal of time. Work finishing the ship's machinery, equipment, and installing armament was hindered and delayed for two years. The observations by the United States of the Japan-Russian war brought about additional changes and alterations in the battleship, utilizing new ideas developed by the war experience.

The greatest change in the construction was the alteration of 12″ gun turrets. When it was found that turrets on the new battleship *Maine* were not heavy enough to withstand the shock of battery,

Nebraska Governor John H. Mickey with Navy Brass.
(courtesy of Rosario Resort)

super-imposed turrets on other ships being built were made heavier. As all those for the *Nebraska* were already made, an idea is gained of the length of time consumed making the changes.

The *Nebraska* contract became long and drawn out, no doubt disappointing to the Morans, who were anxious to finish the project. The U.S. Navy's Inspector of Equipment and later Chief Executive Officer of the *Nebraska*, Lt. Robert E. Coontz, was actively involved with the Morans to complete the ship.

> *"I found the Moran Brothers a strict concern with which to deal. My predecessor had had many disagreements with them, and finally had to be detached. I endeavored to be pleasant. From time to time, our dealings, even to the smallest detail, were in writing.*
>
> *"Work on the ship was delayed, yet the Moran Brothers were excellent boiler builders, and did good work in the engineering department of the Nebraska.*

Miss Mary Nain Mickey, the battleship's sponsor with her father, Nebraska's Governor.
(courtesy of Rosario Resort)

Robert Moran was a sturdy character and strong in his opinions.

> *"The Nebraska had her engine trial run in Puget Sound off Vashon Island, in July, 1906, and the only noteworthy trouble experienced on the trip was the loss of both bower anchors, let go in the windlass house by someone unknown. At the high speed the battleship was making*

Invitation to the launching of the USS NEBRASKA on October 7, 1904 at 2:13 p.m.   (courtesy of Rosario Resort)

USS NEBRASKA launching — October 7, 1904.   (courtesy of Rosario Resort)

Moran Bros. Company

Seattle, Washington

———

OCTOBER 7, 1904

———

LAUNCHING OF THE

UNITED STATES BATTLESHIP

"NEBRASKA"

PROGRAMME

———

12:30 P. M.
Gates Open to the Public.

12:30 P. M. to 1:00 P. M.

MUSIC.

Wagner's First Regiment **Band**

U. S. Marine Band, **Navy Yard**

Meier's Band

U. S. Army Band, Fort Lawton

LUEBEN'S BAND

The musical program will include the new "Nebraska March"
specially composed by Prof. Sol. Asher.

*Official program of the launching of the battleship
NEBRASKA — Oct. 7, 1904.   (courtesy of Rosario Resort)*

*Construction of NEBRASKA continues at dockside.
(courtesy of Rosario Resort)*

*Mounting Gun turrets on the NEBRASKA.
(courtesy of Rosario Resort)*

*View of the Moran Brothers Co., from the deck of the USS
NEBRASKA. (courtesy of the Whatcom County Museum)*

*Guns being installed on the Battleship NEBRASKA.
(courtesy of the Whatcom County Museum)*

Moran women and friends inspecting the ship.
(courtesy of Rosario Resort)

NEBRASKA being painted in drydock before joining President Roosevelt's "Great White Fleet."
(courtesy of Rosario Resort)

The Battleship's pilot house.
(courtesy of Rosario Resort)

the noise of the chains running out the pipes was so great that many aboard thought that one of the boilers had exploded; an amusing incident occurred in the lower pilot house, where two officers attempted to get through one door at the same time, their bodies were jammed together, and after the excitement was over, it is said to have been necessary to pry them apart.

"The Nebraska new and clean was towed over to the Puget Sound Navy Yard on May 31, 1907 and lay there for a month while the Bureau of Navigation was endeavoring to assign officers and crew to her.

"The Nebraska was placed in commission July 1, 1907. She had a full Marine Guard, a complete band, and a few in the Engineers Department, and only two on deck—a quartermaster and a seaman.

"We started to coal the ship the morning after she was commissioned, having only the musicians in the band to do the work.

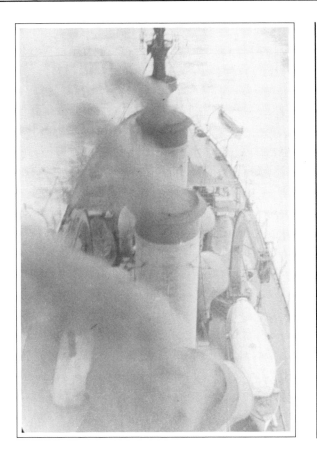

"We greatly needed men to man the ship, and to keep it clean. After some delay, fifty apprentices were sent to us from Mare Island. We had further instructions to enlist our own force. We elected to get them from Washington and Oregon and sent out recruiting parties.

"They were a hard looking crowd when they arrived, but once in a blue jacket's uniform, each man soon took hold, and with their knowledge of seamanship and engine room work helped the Nebraska make the wonderful record she did."

After five years and $3,733,000, the *USS Nebraska* became the last battleship of the "Virginia Class," joining the *Virginia, Georgia, New Jersey*, and *Rhode Island*. The battleship received highest praise from the navy, who felt it was equal to, if not better than, any ship in the world's navies in its day. Every naval officer of that time regarded the *Nebraska* as standing "first in line"—the navy's favorite ship.

The *Nebraska* was 441'3" in length with an extreme beam of 76'3". Her normal displacement tonnage was 14,948 and her draft was 23'9". The ship's normal complement was 40 officers and 772

USS NEBRASKA proving herself off Vashon Island. (courtesy of Rosario Resort)

USS Battleship NEBRASKA, on official trial, July 16, 1906, making 19.518 knots.   (courtesy of Rosario Resort)

Officers and crew of USS NEBRASKA with the Over Seas Fleet during World War I.   (courtesy of Mrs. Patricia Moran)

enlisted men. The *Nebraska's* main armament was four 12″–40's, eight 8″–45's and twelve 6″–50's. Her secondary battery consisted of twelve 3″–50's and eight .30 calibers. To top off this mixture she also had four 21″ submerged torpedo tubes. She carried 1,969 tons of coal in her bunkers and had a design speed of 19 knots.

The *Nebraska* was first sent to San Francisco where she began her cruise around the world with the "Great White Fleet." She acted in the protection of American interests off Vera Cruz during 1914 and 1916, then served throughout World War I as a training ship for Armed Guard crews. The ship was often the escort of fast mercantile convoys from the eastern seaboard to ocean rendezvous with armed ships, which in turn safeguarded them to ports off England and France. At the close of World War I she made four voyages from Virginia ports to Brest, France for the return of 4,540 American troops.

By 1923, the *Nebraska* had become obsolete and was "rendered incapable of further warlike service" by the Treaty Limiting Naval Armament. She was dismantled and sold for $37,100 to a California scrap metal dealer. This was a respectable ending compared to the other ships of her class, most of which were destroyed by U.S. Navy target practice during World War I.

Orcas Island Yesterdays

After the *Nebraska* launching in 1904, the strain of a lifetime of hard work, full responsibility for managing the family corporation, and the complexities of the battleship contract had taken their toll on Robert Moran, both mentally and physically. He wintered in Santa Barbara, California in 1905, and thereafter made several trips to consult with European specialists. On their advice, in 1906 at age 49, he decided to retire from active business. This ended a period of thirty years in the activities of Seattle's business life. The Moran Brothers Company, which had increased in value up in the millions of dollars, had become a Seattle institution. It was sold in March of 1906 to Eastern capitalists, Breton, Griscom, and Jenks, who reorganized under the name The Moran Company. In 1912 it became Seattle Construction and Drydock, and in 1916 Todd Shipyards purchased the plant, then moved to a new location in 1918. Today, the Kingdome sits atop the original Moran Brothers Company location.

In 1904, the doctors had issued me a ticket for a permanent residence in Lakeview Cemetery, Seattle, for the reason that they predicted that I had organic heart disease. Thirty-four years ago, the medical profession was not as well informed on heart disease as it is today. My real trouble was a highly nervous condition brought on by a badly overworked physical and mental life, due to the fact that the entire finance and general superintendence of the Moran Brothers Company shipbuilding business was on me. It must be remembered that the company was a close family corporation with no interest held outside the Moran family. That condition affected the heart's action and deceived the doctors, as is proved now thirty-five years after, when at eighty-two years, the old pump seems to be giving perfect hydraulic service.

However, it is not to be denied that I was a worn down man physically, who particularly needed mental rest. This led me to the decision to dispose of the Seattle shipbuilding property and retire to Orcas Island. That movement gave me

Moran at retirement.   (courtesy of Rosario Resort)

particularly mental rest from business cares, though I had to continue in construction work in the planning of the building of Rosario.

Moran Retires to Orcas Island

During a pleasure cruise through the San Juan Islands shortly after the doctor's gloomy edict, Moran visited Orcas Island at the time when a Captain Newhall operated a small sawmill on Cascade Bay. Moran soon realized the slow, tranquil life of the islands could renew his failing health. He became intrigued with Newhall's set-up, for here was a location which already had various working buildings plus terrain ideal for hydroelectric development.

In 1905 Moran bought the Cascade Lumber and Manufacturing Company, which was incorporated in 1887 to manufacture barrel stock for Orcas Island lime works, boxes, and dressed and rough lumber for local trade. The officers of the company were brothers, E.P. Newhall, president, and

The Cascade Lumber and Manufacturing Company — 1905.   (courtesy of the Whatcom County Museum)

Andrew Newhall, superintendent. A small work force of ten was employed at the company, which also was equipped with a steamboat and tug.

The date 1888 is attributed to the Andrew Newhall house, the only remaining structure of the Newhall enterprise. The Moran family occupied this residence during the planning and construction of the main mansion at Rosario. A note by Mrs. Moran in the original guest register documents the family took up residence in the mansion on June 21, 1909.

Robert Moran began acquiring the surrounding land very secretly through various agents. One colorful character he bought out was a Mrs. Cox who ran a small hotel on Cascade Lake. After her hotel burned down she lived alone in what many considered a "solitary paradise." She raised her own vegetables and fruit, and would rake trout from the lake and put them in a live box until she was ready to eat them. She had also located a gold mine on her property and, when she sold to Moran, reserved her right to work the mine. She moved east, never to return, and the gold mine still makes many people wonder . . .

Moran eventually acquired 7800 acres of Orcas Island, consisting of four fresh water lakes, Mt. Constitution, the sawmill, a postoffice (established in 1890) and a schoolhouse. The postoffice was originally called "Newhall," after the first owner, but was changed to "Rosario" on June 15, 1906. The new name was adopted from Rosario Strait, which separates the San Juan Islands from the mainland. Originally named by Spanish explorers

Cascade Bay before Moran began construction of Rosario.   (courtesy of Betty Moran Burns)

1905

The Morans outside the Newhall house in 1905.
(courtesy of Rosario Resort)

in 1791 as the ''Gran Canal de Nuestra Senora del Rosario la Marinera,'' its title was too long for navigational charts and later shortened to simply Rosario Strait. Moran liked the charm, ring and sound of the name Rosario and used it for his estate.

The San Juan Islands

In the lower reaches of Puget Sound and the Gulf of Georgia, looking out through the Strait of Juan de Fuca, toward the indles and lands of romance on the chief trade routes of the world's future commerce, lies a land unique and apart from anything else in the Western Hemisphere—the San Juan Islands.

Unique in charm and beauty, in perfection of climate, in easy, agreeable living conditions, in healthfulness; unique in the fact that it is an entire county of sea and land, of islands and inlets, 172 in number, varying in size from 58 square miles to the area of a city lot.

The San Juan Islands are known as the ''Sunshine Belt,'' due to the fact that the rain-laden clouds sweeping in from the Pacific through the Straits pass over the Islands frequently without precipitating their moisture until they encounter the high snow barriers of the Cascade and Olympic Mountains.

It is a wonderful place in which to

San Juan Islands with Mt. Baker in the distance.
(courtesy of Betty Moran Burns)

The Moran brothers and family out yachting.   (courtesy of Rosario Resort)

forget one's troubles and worries and get back to Nature in her happiest moods; a delightful place in which to regain health—physical, mental and spiritual.

The San Juan Archipelago actually represent tops of a submerged mountain range that once crossed Puget Sound in an east-west direction from Vancouver Island to the Continent. During a time long past, these mountains were covered with glaciers, and the rock formation of the islands is mostly a sedimentary, waterlaid, fossil-bearing limestone and shale with traces of plutonic, or "fire" rock. Trees that fringe the shores of the San Juans are spruce, hemlock, cedar, yew, juniper, madrona, oak, dogwood, and douglas fir, which resemble Japanese Cypress as they lean out over the water. What at one time were 600 to 1,000 ft. canyons are now the many waterways where ferries, private yachts and sailboats cruise, and where yesterday trading and exploring schooners and Indian dugouts came and went.

When Spanish explorers came in 1791, the islands had been hunting grounds of the peaceful Lummi tribe for many generations. There are no predatory animals on the islands, so the area was rich with food. Local Lummi tribes feared the not-so-friendly Northern Indians who came to hunt

and fish their rich islands during summer months. War-like Haidas from as far north as the Queen Charlotte Islands, and half a dozen other tribes from mainland British Columbia, made life a bit unpleasant for the Lummi tribe—putting to work any natives they happened upon. A certain area was allotted to each tribe as their "summer home," where they fished and smoked their catch for the coming winter, then departed, leaving the Lummi tribe to hunt and fish the San Juans themselves during the winter.

Spanish explorers arriving in 1791 were Captain Francisco Eliza and his two Lieutenants, Fidalgo and Quimper. They did a creditable job in charting the islands considering the primitive methods by which their work was done. Besides naming Rosario Strait, they named the islands of San Juan, Decatur, Lopez, Fidalgo, Orcas and "Isla and Archipelago de San Juan."

There are two theories behind the naming of Orcas Island. The first and most widely accepted was an attempt by Captain Eliza to honor the Viceroy of Mexico, whose full name was Don Juan Vicente de Guemes Pacheco y Padilla *Orcasitees y Aguayo Conde de Revilla Gigedo.*

But the more romantic version is that the original name of the island was "Isla de Orcas" in honor of the Blackfish. Orca is the Spanish word

Original Eastsound dock. (courtesy of Rosario Resort)

for Grampus and Blackfish, or killer whale as they are most often called. It is not beyond all probability that Captain Eliza happened upon a school of Orca playing in around the island and named it for them.

In 1792, Captain George Vancouver arrived in time to bestow the names of many of his British friends in and around the archipelago. The name of his second lieutenant, Peter Puget, was given to the sound, the largest land-locked body of water in the United States. The tallest peak in Washington he named after Admiral Rainer and its neighbor to the north on the Cascade Range in honor of his third lieutenant, Joseph Baker.

A scientific expedition by Congress in 1841 was commanded by Captain Charles Wilkes, who proceeded to rename all the islands in the archipelago with naval names. Fortunately Wilkes' system of naming the islands was poorly executed and only a few names remain today, including Mt. Constitution, named after the U.S. frigate *Constitution.*

The first white settlers began to arrive on the islands in the mid-1800's, with the Lummi Indians never really giving them much trouble. The only real incident that occurred during the settlement of the islands was not between the Indians and the Whites, but between the Americans and the British.

The Pig War

The international boundary had been defined in the Boundary Line Treaty of 1846 as running along the 49th parallel of latitude "to the middle of the channel which separates the continent from Vancouver's island and thence southerly, through the middle of the said channel and of Fuca's strait, to the Pacific Ocean." This indefinite wording led the British to believe that the "said channel" was Rosario Strait, between Orcas Island and the mainland, and the Americans to believe it was the

Canal de Haro, which runs between San Juan and Vancouver's Island.

The British-owned Hudson's Bay Company established the very successful "Bellevue Farm" on San Juan Island in 1853. The Hudson's Bay Company had several thousand sheep and many horses, cattle, and pigs with Hawaiian sheepherders hired by the British to work their farm. Nearby, 25 American settlers began homesteading and working their farms. These citizens of the new Washington Territory, which separated from Oregon in 1853, believed this land was theirs. A dispute between Governor Isaac J. Stevens of Washington Territory and Governor James Douglas of Vancouver's island had gone on for years, but both were warned by their national governments not to get too tough.

In 1859 a gunshot echoed through the evergreens when Lyman A. Cutler, an American settler, shot a British pig that was rooting up his potato patch. That one and only shot began an international incident that lasted for years, known as the "pig war."

A reimbursement of $100 was offered for the unlucky pig, but refused by the British, after which the Americans armed themselves with rifles to save Cutler from being shipped off to Victoria for trial. Brigadier General William E. Harney was informed by the San Juan residents that they were in danger of "hostile Indians," so he dispatched Captain George E. Pickett (Battle of Gettysburg fame) with 68 infantrymen to San Juan Island for the defense of the Americans. When the British learned of an American military landing, three warships were sent and threatened to land troops from the ships, but Captain Pickett stated he would resist to the last man.

After level headed Governors and Generals became involved with the incident, which soon involved 2,600 men, 170 cannon, and 5 warships, a joint occupation by British and American troops

"Mother-in-law" on street in Friday Harbor.
(courtesy of Rosario Resort)

was proposed, pending diplomatic settlement. In March of 1860, a detachment of 100 Royal Marines landed on the north end of San Juan Island and set up English Camp, with the Americans reducing their troops to the same number in the American Camp on the south end.

Finally in 1872, Emperor Kaiser Wilhelm I of Germany, who had been chosen to arbitrate the dispute, decided that the boundary line ran through Canal de Haro to the west where the water is 100 to 190 fathoms deep instead of Rosario Strait to the east where it is less than 50 fathoms deep.

So ended the ''pig war,'' with the only casualty being—a pig. The Americans won the romantic group of islands and the British accepted the verdict with good sportsmanship. A year later the islands were organized by the Territorial Legislature of Washington into the local governmental entity of San Juan County.

Moran listening to President Roosevelt at the University of Washington — 1909.   (courtesy of Betty Moran Burns)

Rosario Yesterdays

R obert Moran approached the development of Rosario with the same thoroughness and zeal he had applied to his business. Constructing his home was a labor of love for good craftsmanship, by a man who was accustomed to building ships that could withstand the worst the Pacific Ocean had to offer. Everything was built massively, and with no expense spared in making Rosario one of the most substantial homes on the Pacific Coast.

The Building of Rosario

Building Rosario was simply a continuance of my life-long urge to be continually pushing ahead on industrial construction work.

At first, plans for a two-story house of frame construction by a professional architect were commissioned but these were laid aside. Moran himself designed the mansion, and thereafter oversaw the entire construction of every portion of the home. Construction began in 1906, with Moran's oldest son, John M., serving as his father's construction foreman. Moran transformed the buildings of the Cascade Lumber Co. into shops in which metals and imported whole hardwood logs could be worked on the site. Expert craftsman Ernest Miller was in charge of woodworking. At times, fifty to sixty workmen, most of whom were former Moran Bros. Co. shipwrights, were on the payroll at $1.75 for a ten-hour day. Moran used only the finest craftsmen available, and if he found someone whose work he particularly liked, but had nothing at the time for him to construct, he would quickly think of something just to keep him under his employ.

Before actual construction of the mansion, Moran began developing the estate to be self-sufficient for its power and water. He built his own D.C. hydroelectric power system to run his shop motors, then later to supply electricity for Rosario's electric lights, cooking, refrigeration, and laundry equipment. Moran's project also created sufficient power to heat the entire mansion, one of the earliest homes anywhere to be electrically heated.

To furnish the power, a log dam at Cascade Lake (350 ft. above Cascade Bay) was built to raise the water level, but later had to be replaced by a concrete dam and supplemented by yet another dam and artificial water flow from Mountain Lake at a higher elevation of 914 ft. A concrete power house is located by the lagoon, and still supplies 125 kilo-

Moran Mansion and estate grounds overlooking East Sound. The mansion has 5 floors, including the lower level and attic, with 54 rooms overall — 18 of which were bedrooms.   (courtesy of Betty Moran Burns)

Part of the Rosario waterfront, showing the concrete power house and three story concrete shop and storage building in the distance. The machine shop and warehouse building housed fully equipped machine, metal and woodworking shops, a brass foundry and electric welding and gas equipment. A stock of general mechanical merchandise and a supply of lumber were also stored in the building. Although the date inscribed on the south gable is 1925, it is known that most of the custom work required to outfit and furnish the mansion was carried out in this building, or on its site, between 1906 and 1912.
(courtesy of Betty Moran Burns)

watts to power the outside lights and to heat the mansion. A larger power house was built in 1921, to add room for an auxiliary diesel generator.

A never failing spring on the estate flows from the base of Mt. Constitution, at an elevation of 700 ft. This was piped to a concrete reservoir buried in the ground at an elevation of about 100 ft., which insured a pure water supply at Rosario for all domestic purposes. Lake water was used for irrigation.

A machine shop and warehouse building was completed before the mansion and from it came the bronze castings of hinges, door fasteners and all other innumerable hardware that is found throughout the building. In 1925, Moran rebuilt this machine shop into a solid concrete, three story building, and like everything he built, it was made to last.

The woodwork for the mansion was largely constructed from timber brought to the island in log from around the world. Thoroughly seasoned after cutting, it was then worked into final shape by the shipwrights and artisans. The majority of finished woods in the interior are Indian teak and

Honduran mahogany. The teak was used for basketweave parqueted flooring throughout the home, taking craftsmen two years to complete. The

Lower level laundry room featured the latest in laundry facilities.   *(courtesy of Rosario Resort*

Billiard room on lower level of the mansion. Tables were built atop a portion of sculpted solid rock. Lower level flooring consists of Italian mosaic tile.
(courtesy of Betty Moran Burns)

flooring was laid with 5/8 inch steel brads and glued with tongue and groove 2x6 kiln dried fir. This was sanded off to a smooth surface and another layer of tongue and grooved 1x4 kiln dried fir was glued, which was again sanded and laid with the 3/8 inch thick parquet teakwood. Mahogany was used for paneling, doors, door and window trim, and ceiling beams of the mansion.

The mansion itself reflects Moran's nautical design and building experience. While the structure is highly individual in character, it bears a distinct relationship to the Arts and Crafts movement, a style advanced in this country by Gustav Stickley's magazine *The Craftsmen*, which began publication in 1901. Stickley's principles of the ''craftsmen'' home were ''simplicity, durability, fitness for the life that is to be lived in the house and harmony with its natural surroundings,'' a unique reflection of Moran's Rosario.

The mansion foundation was blasted out of 16 feet of solid bedrock, with the lower level, first and second floors constructed of ten inch, steel reinforced concrete. The third floor and attic are of frame construction, with the roof originally having a cedar shake cover, but later being overlaid with 6 tons of copper sheeting when Moran acquired a large supply at a reduced rate during the depression.

The exterior of the mansion was painted by Moran with a maroon paint, but it was later painted white by the second owners. The maroon paint was actually shipbottom paint . . . the builder obviously had a few gallons left over!

Each floor is 6600 sq. ft., with the lower level primarily a recreation area. Lower level flooring consists of varicolored Italian mosaic tile. The game room featured a billiard table, pool table, and a two-lane bowling alley. In the adjoining gymnasium is a 13x40 ft. swimming pool which was originally saltwater and tile-lined. A laundry and furnace room were also located on the lower level as well as a vault, containing two large manganese time-lock safes.

The main floor comprises a veranda that entirely surrounds the home, the stairhall, a 30x39 ft. living-dining room, the kitchen and pantries, and two large refrigeration rooms, one for chilling and one for freezing.

The living-dining room features the rich Honduran mahogany and teak woodwork reminiscent of ship's carpentry, frosted hemispherical shiplight globes in ''port hole'' mounts and a massive molded concrete fireplace with inlaid polished marble chips. The fireplace mantel was cast in one piece by the Moran Company and shipped to Rosario for installation, with the marble chips being from Seattle's old Union Depot. The supply of fireplace wood for the mansion was from driftwood on the beaches. No forest wood on the estate was cut by Moran for that purpose.

Two lane maple bowling alley — lower level. It was laid atop steel beams imbedded in the rock foundation.
(courtesy of Rosario Resort)

The original 13 x 40 ft. saltwater indoor pool. Tile lined, it is located in the lower level.   (courtesy of Rosario Resort)

The living-dining room, featuring teak dining tables and leather rockers.   (courtesy of Rosario Resort)

The massive fireplace mantel in the living-dining room is molded concrete.   (courtesy of Rosario Resort)

Windows throughout the mansion are 7/8 inch Belgian plate glass. They pivot on special Moran designed brass devices mounted at the center of the casements, resulting in a louvre effect. Italian marbelized colored glass is above the windows, with the electric heating system behind copper lattice work below the windows.
(courtesy of Rosario Resort)

Butterfly hinge   (courtesy of Rosario Resort)

The windows of the mansion are long, narrow bays of 7/8 inch Belgian plate glass used for ship's glass. There were no pictures on walls of the home, for Moran felt that "at Rosario you view the outside beauties of nature through Belgian plate glass." Lighting in the home was provided not only by the direct shiplight fixtures, but also by indirect lighting over ribbon windows and doors. The light-ing is diffused through plates of marbelized colored glass imported from Italy.

There are several hundred mahogany doors in the mansion, each one so thick and heavy that special hinges were designed and built for them by Moran. The special bronze "butterfly" hinges contain carved double cone shaped pins of lignum vitae. A hardwood that sinks in water, lignum vitae produces natural oils which lubricate the hinges. The wood was often used by shipbuilders below water lines and for packing shafts to lubricate the bearings.

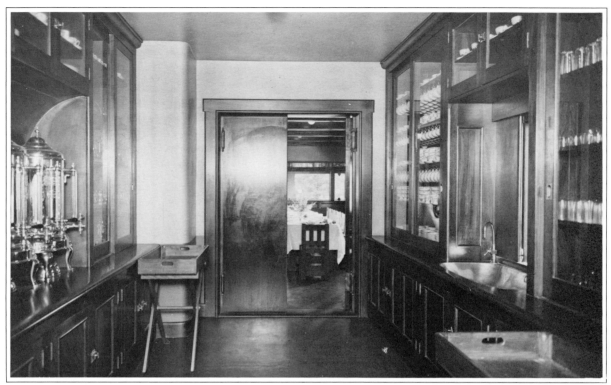

Pantry room adjoining the dining area. It contains a complete stock of utensils for "elegant" dining and two large copper coffee urns.   (courtesy of Rosario Resort)

The kitchen, with completely electrically equipped ranges, refrigeration and water heating.(courtesy of Rosario Resort)

Kitchen showing cold storage rooms and ice machine. (courtesy of Rosario Resort)

Staff dining area off the kitchen.
(courtesy of Rosario Resort)

The tall teak clock in the main stair hall landing with a beaten copper face and a plate glass door revealing the assorted polished brass eights was built with the mansion. Another case clock is located in the Music Room and was built in 1913 by the Herschel Clock Co. of Cincinnati, Ohio.
(courtesy of Rosario Resort)

The front hall and grand stair case of the Moran Mansion.
(courtesy of Rosario Resort)

The second floor of the home is comprised of a music room, twelve bedrooms, a trunk or utility room, a sporting goods room, a sewing room and a linen room. The third floor features the balcony of the music room with twin libraries, a photo dark room, dispensary and seven bedrooms. To top it all off, there is a large attic that was capable of sleeping fifty people on cots.

The focal point of Rosario, and the room that was Robert Moran's pride, is the music room, for it boasts many specially acquired features. Among them is a hexagonal stained glass light fixture depicting the seven liberal arts. It is attributed, on the basis of Moran's correspondence, to Louis Comfort Tiffany, that paragon of Arts and Crafts ideals. On the eighth panel of the work a poem called ''Opportunity'' appears. Written in 1891 by a Republican Senator from Kansas named John James Ingalls, the poem's setting reflects Moran's own opportunities after arriving on the Seattle waterfront at 17 years of age with a dime in his pocket.

The Moran Music Room features a 26 rank Aeolian ''player'' pipe organ. Exposed pipes are simply facade — the real 1,972 pipes are hidden behind mahogany lattice work.   *(courtesy of the Whatcom County Museum)*

Second floor hallway featuring rich Honduran Mahogany paneling and teak parquet flooring.
(courtesy of Betty Moran Burns)

OPPORTUNITY

MASTER OF HUMAN DESTINIES AM I!
FAME, LOVE AND FORTUNE ON MY
   FOOTSTEPS WAIT.
CITIES AND FIELDS I WALK —
I PENETRATE DESERTS AND SEAS REMOTE,
AND PASSING BY HOVEL AND MARTLAND
   PALACE — SOON OR LATE,
I KNOCK UNBIDDEN ONCE ON EVERY GATE!
IF SLEEPING, WAKE —
IF FEASTING, RISE,
BEFORE I TURN AWAY.
IT IS THE HOUR OF FATE,
AND THEY WHO FOLLOW ME REACH
   EVERY STATE.
MORTALS DESIRE, AND CONQUER EVERY FOE
   SAVE DEATH,
BUT THOSE WHO DOUBT OR HESITATE,
CONDEMN TO FAILURE, PENURY AND WOE.
SEEK ME IN VAIN AND USELESSLY IMPLORE,
I ANSWER NOT, AND RETURN NO MORE!

JOHN JAMES INGALLS 1891

A second piece of stained glass art in the room is a large clerestory window which depicts in detail the harbor in Antwerp, chief port of Belgium. The painted and etched glass work shows various steamers and sailing ships in the harbor, and major landmarks on the east bank of the Scheldt, including the Cathedral of the Holy Virgin, the late medieval fortress and the Stadhuis, or townhall. The work is signed by ''L. de Contini, Brussels, Belgium,'' from whom Moran commissioned the work especially for the mansion.

A large fireplace on the entrance wall of the

Opposite view of music room from the bay windows looking toward the entrance.
(courtesy of the Whatcom County Museum)

room is faced with green ceramic tile and trimmed with studded copper. Sailing ships are depicted in blue and white tile above the mantel, and marine lanterns accent each side.

The highlight feature of the music room is the 26 rank Aeolian pipe organ, installed in 1913. The original cost of the organ was $16,000 and it contains 1,972 pipes. The pipes take up almost half the room, located in wind chambers concealed behind beautiful hand-latticed mahogany and a facade of artificial organ pipes. The organ console is hidden above the main floor in a horseshoe shaped balcony, reminiscent of a ship's ballroom. The organ is actually a ''player'' organ, and like a player piano, operates on music rolls. The

Music room from the balcony features a Tiffany chandelier and stained glass window depicting the harbor at Antwerp, Belgium.

(courtesy of Rosario Resort)

One side of the Moran library in Music Room balcony, featuring a teakwood desk with economy of space.
(courtesy of Rosario Resort)

original console had no keyboard, simply the "stops" or presets used to operate a rank of pipes. In later years the console was rebuilt by the W.W. Kimball Co. to include a two manual keyboard for manual operation.

Despite not being able to play a note, Mr. Moran invited island residents and estate guests to organ concerts in which he presided "at the keyboard." Only his back from the waist up was visible from the floor below, and his guests, actually believing that he was playing, congratulated him on wonderful concerts!

The music room also contains a beautiful ornate 1900 Steinway grand piano and a small harmonium, or pump organ, which is located in the balcony.

The Moran libraries are in twin alcoves on opposite sides of the balcony, featuring many first edition, turn–of–the–century volumes—reference, professional, and fiction—as well as numerous history sets and eycyclopedias. Matching high polished teak desks are located in each library. Designed after nautical chart desks, Moran used the numerous drawers for his own plate glass and stereoptigon photograph collection.

As were the nautical chart desks, most of the furniture in the mansion is of highly polished teak, built by the shipwrights as the mansion was being

Moran's nautical influence is evident in lighting fixtures throughout the home, including marine lanterns above the music room fireplace (above), and a bedroom table lamp (right).
(courtesy of the Whatcom County Museum)

(courtesy of Rosario Resort)

Captain Tuttle, retired from the Coast Guard, then called the Revenue Cutter Service, went to spend the weekend with the Morans and stayed eight years until his death! Captain Tuttle always said he slept best in the cabin of the cutter BEAR, so Moran built a shipsbunk in his guest room.
(courtesy of Rosario Resort)

Typical bedroom containing Moran designed solid teak bureau, with two swinging brass frames supporting four mirrors.
(courtesy of the Whatcom County Museum)

A typical bath — there were six in the residence. Most of the fixtures were very advanced for the day, similar to equipment used by spas and resorts of the period.
(courtesy of Rosario Resort)

"Arts and Crafts" style conversation chairs designed by Moran.　　　(courtesy of Rosario Resort)

View from third floor hallway into the Music Room Balcony. A projection booth was added at this spot by the second owner in the late 1930's.　　(courtesy of Rosario Resort)

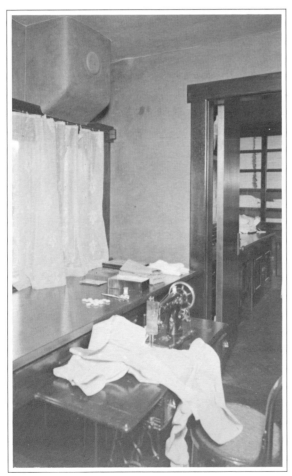

The sewing room and linen storage room.
　　　(courtesy of Rosario Resort)

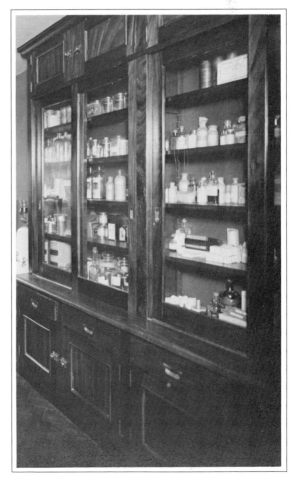

The dispensary, for there were no drug stores on Orcas Island.　　　(courtesy of Rosario Resort)

The large well-finished attic, capable of sleeping 50 people on cots. (courtesy of Rosario Resort)

constructed. Also designed in the Arts and Crafts style, or so-called "Mission Style," the furniture is of sound construction and straight line; banquet tables, chairs, dressers with revolving mirror stands, built-in ship's bunks and an extensive assembly of built-in kitchen and pantry cabinetry.

Although small fireplaces are in all rooms on the second floor, they proved inefficient, so small portable D.C. heaters replaced the burning wood. This was in addition to the electric heating system of the larger rooms, which consisted of D.C. powered copper heating elements that were located behind brass lattice work. In the case of an occasional cold spell, an oil furnace also supplied heat to the home.

Landscaping of the estate was held to a minimum, for it was Moran's intent to retain as much of the natural setting as possible. A high-grade rolled lawn was maintained in the small court created by a circular carriage drive fronting the mansion. At the carriage circle entrance, Moran strung anchor chain—originally from the *USS Nebraska*—between pedestals for tethering horses. When the *Nebraska* was making her trial run, one of the U.S.N. officers required that the anchor chain be "run-out" free while the ship was going at 19 knots. Moran protested, saying that no one would anchor a boat while at full speed. They insisted on the test and the chain ran out across the deck into the water until it caught on a pipe and broke in two. The U.S.N. disgarded the remainder, which Moran acquired for Rosario, and the lost chain lies somewhere in Puget Sound.

A fountain for watering horses was placed in front of the chain, with a concrete carriage and utility house located next to the mansion. Pathways wound through gardens and orchards from the mansion to the estate shops. Next to the power house Moran built a 360 ft. long concrete lagoon for his wife to swim and canoe in. The water was circulated fresh, moving through the hydroelectric waterwheels from Cascade Lake to Cascade Bay. The lagoon, featuring islands on either end and a concrete arch bridge, was built in 1915. One year later, a ship's figurehead was added to grace the lawn between lagoon and waterfront. This sculpture was from the clipper ship *America*,

Circular carriage drive with horse watering fountain and USS NEBRASKA anchor chain used as horse hitch.
(courtesy of Rosario Resort)

Rosario Estate's formal gardens with the Moran Brothers' homes in the background.
(courtesy of the Whatcom County Museum)

A fresh water lagoon was built for canoeing and swimming. (courtesy of Rosario Resort)

salvaged by Moran after the ship was wrecked on San Juan Island. The *America* had been used for trade between San Francisco and Liverpool in previous years, and Moran placed the figurehead to greet the many sailors to his port.

Lining all pathways of the estate are electric cluster lights, which burn constantly on the D.C. generator. These lights were old Seattle street lamps that Moran acquired, and when darkness falls, the play of outdoor lighting on the water and around the mansion and grounds make Rosario seem like a festive oasis indeed.

There was a 40x162 ft. "side-hill" barn located near the entrance of the estate. Built very much like the mansion, with blasted solid rock foundation and steel reinforced concrete construction

The figurehead from the clipper ship AMERICA.
(courtesy of the Whatcom County Museum)

INSCRIPTION ON FIGUREHEAD
This figurehead is from the clipper ship "America." She was built in 1874 at Quincy, Massachusetts by Deacon George Thomas. Her original owners were Thayer & Co. of Boston. In 1887 she was put in the Pacific coasting trade and was wrecked on San Juan Island in the year 1914. The "America" has some notable voyages to her credit. Namely, from New York to San Francisco in 89 days and from San Francisco to Liverpool in 102 days. Captain J.S. Gibson, at one time her commander, records that this figurehead was a source of much pride to him, that it had many times in many ports been remarked upon as being one of the most artistic figureheads that ever graced the bow of a ship and there is probably no other on an American vessel that has been mentioned so many times in public print. It is carved from a solid white pine log. This is erected by me to commemorate a beautiful sentiment in ship building now becoming a lost art. Figure donated by Captain James Griffiths.
Rosario 1916   Robert Moran

on the lower level, the barn was designed so a wagon could be driven into any one of the three levels. The lower level was fitted for cows, the second for horses and vehicles, and the third for forage and farm and garden implements. The barn burned in later years and was never rebuilt. Across the entrance drive from the barn location is an earth-covered concrete fruit and vegetable house which insured the safe keeping of produce.

A school was located on the Olga road just south of Cascade Lake, but was closed after most of the area residents moved away. Moran established a school for his and his workmen's children above the first machine shop, but with all the machinery

Seattle street lamps which Moran placed along sidewalks throughout the estate. NEBRASKA anchor chain connects these lamps in front of mansion.
(courtesy of Rosario Resort)

noise, this experiment did not last long. A new school was built—with accommodations for the teacher—on the hill above the fruit and vegetable house, but has long since been torn down.

A circular concrete "playhouse" was built in 1914 overlooking Cascade Bay. With cooks and servants in the main household, Moran felt his family needed a "get-away" spot in which to gather and learn domestic chores on their own. Daughter Nellie was able to learn cooking and canning in the roundhouse kitchen, while son Malcolm had his own ceramic kiln and lathe to pursue his interests in pottery.

Since Moran did not allow housing of his domestic staff in the mansion itself, additional living quarters were built on the estate. Sitting in the trees immediately west of the estate's access road on the slope above the mansion were two rustic Craftsmen bungalows, with peeled log porch posts. A larger cottage to the left was for the maids, while a smaller one housed the cook. Across Cascade Bay from the mansion was the gardener's home.

Two of Robert's brothers, Frank and Sherman, had decided to build homes on the estate, but in

Hillside three story barn which has vehicle access on any floor. Lower level was for cows, second for horses and vehicles, and the top for fodder and implements. A manure storage tank appears at right.
(courtesy of Betty Moran Burns)

The solid concrete "playhouse," equipped with kitchen.
(courtesy of Betty Moran Burns)

Frank and Sherman Morans' identical homes.
(courtesy of Betty Moran Burns)

Daily visits were made to Rosario by the mail and passenger boat "ROSALIE."
(courtesy of the Whatcom County Museum)

the planning stages of the new homes, the brothers' wives made it competitive. It seems they were always trying to "outdo" each other, and when it came time for new homes, one wife wanted the nicer home, the other a bigger home, one the nicer yard, the other the better view, until the brothers put an end to the problem. They built the exact same house twice—right next door to each other—same yard, same view! Also Craftsmen style bungalows, the pair of three-story homes are located on the slope above the lagoon.

Rosario was remote from hectic urban life, but by no means isolated. It was connected to the Pacific Telephone and Telegraph lines on the mainland via a five mile private hookup to the Eastsound office. Moreover, ferry service was maintained as a two-daily trip between Anacortes on mainland Washington and Vancouver Island to Orcas Island. There was also daily mail service from Seattle and Bellingham to Rosario, aboard the mail and passenger ship *Rosalie*. The revenue from the Rosario postoffice, which had its own postmaster, provided free post and parcel post service to the estate.

Robert Moran and Captain Tuttle with prize catch.
(Above and right)   *(courtesy of Rosario Resort)*

(courtesy of Rosario Resort)

Over steps of the northeast end a watch bell inscribed
"Rosario," and behind are red, green and white marine
lanterns which decorate entrance to the living-dining
room.

(courtesy of Betty Moran Burns)

Showplace of the San Juans

Upon completion, Rosario was called the "Showplace of the San Juan Islands." By 1911, Moran had acquired 7,800 acres, with a total cost of development for Rosario estimated at $1,500,000. The style of life at Rosario was rustic—in the most elegant sense of the term. Moran was hospitable and no doubt enjoyed receiving the guests, who made their way to Orcas Island from Seattle and other parts of the world by private yacht. It was an eighty mile trip by inland water route from Seattle; nevertheless, the estate was not developed to be a showplace but a means of absorbing Moran's constructive tendencies and gainfully employing others in the process.

Robert Moran did take great pleasure in opening the estate to visitors every Thursday, but some of these abused their privileges by "taking" souvenirs. Story has it that the open houses ended when a woman was caught taking a bath in Mrs. Moran's private bathroom.

Moran, who always wore suits, would often greet curious boaters at the marina as he was walking his dogs. Often asked by the boaters if he had seen "Mr. Moran," and claiming they were his close friends, Moran would reply "I think he went up there," then point to the mansion and go on with his walk.

The Morans entertained extensively and many friends came from Seattle to spend one or two days at the estate. With plenty of extra guest rooms, they were able to accommodate many overnight. However, guests would have to put up with one famous Moran tradition. Every morning at 7 a.m., Robert would sneak up to the music room balcony and awake the household with the player pipe organ, often playing "Work for the night is Coming."

The household was run like a ship, with breakfast at 7:30 a.m. sharp, lunch at noon, and dinner at six. Red, green and white ship's lanterns greeted guests as they entered the dining room from outside, as well as watch bell inscribed "Rosario," which was rung for emergencies only.

A variety of leisure-time activities could be pursued at Rosario, including horseback riding, hiking,

Robert Moran and Edmond Meany.
(courtesy of Betty Moran Burns)

camping, trout fishing, swimming and croquet on the rear lawn. Wild deer grazed in the orchards, from antlered buck to timid fawn, but gave little attention to visitors as they passed by on the way from dock to mansion.

One of Moran's close and long-time friends was University of Washington Professor Edmond Meany. Both were members of the Mountaineers, and the Morans often hosted the outing club at Rosario. Ed Meany, historian, geographer, meteorologist and botanist, shared many of the same interests as Robert Moran, mainly as a friend to nature and the American Indian. Both had traveled with Edward Curtis (brother of Asahel, whose photographs appear in this volume), famed photographer of the Native Americans. Upon his first visit to Rosario, Meany composed this poem for his good friend Robert Moran:

ORCAS ISLAND

Near ocean's gate in love doth wait
Thy arms to welcome home;
Aye, soon or late, o joyous fate,
Thy sailors homeward come.
How heart throbs yearn
For tides that turn
Fow'rd island shore near ocean's gate!

Thy green hills tower, they symbol power,
O'erlooking foreign land,
Thy bastion's glower is here a flower
And trees as soldiers stand.
Ah peace still hedge
Our nations edge,
While thou doth watch the day's
     last hour!

I love each tree, I hail with glee
Thy very pebbled beach.
My spirit free doth learn of thee
What leaves and birds may teach.
O mile our shore
Forevermore,
Fair Orcas, Queen of Sunset Sea.

Edmond S. Meany
Nov. 16, 1909

Moran State Park

Moran often took his guests on afternoon carriage rides to the top of Mt. Constitution.

Mount Constitution, 2405 ft. high, has

Mount Baker from top of Mt. Constitution in Moran State Park, at an elevation of 2405 ft.
(courtesy of Betty Moran Burns)

Carriage ride to the summit of Mt. Constitution.
(courtesy of Betty Moran Burns)

*a panoramic view of sea and islands
framed in a setting of snow-clad
mountains that, as a picture of sheer
beauty, has no earthly superior. Probably
it is too near Seattle to be interesting —
people like to travel far for their scenic
thrills . . .*

In 1911, Moran attempted to donate 2998 of his
acres to the State of Washington as the "Moran
State Park." The state declined the generous offer,
and it wasn't until 1921, and with great per-
sistence from Mr. Moran, that the state finally
accepted this offer. The land, originally acquired
at about $5 an acre, included Mt. Constitution,
with its 360° panorama of the San Juan Islands,
Strait of Georgia, Rosario Strait, Cascade Range on
mainland Washington, Canadian Coastal Range of
British Columbia and the Olympic Peninsula to the
south, four mountain lakes, and a wealth of wood-
land and greenery.

After dedication of the park, Moran built miles
of roads and trails, concrete bridges, and gateway
arches over the road at the boundaries of the
park—all at his own cost. From the summit, the
view effect of Mt. Constitution was heightened

Entrance arch to Moran State Park.
(courtesy of Betty Moran Burns)

Olga Road bridge Moran built in Moran State Park.
(courtesy of Betty Moran Burns)

Moran built steel-concrete bridge on the park road to
Mountain Lake.   (courtesy of Betty Moran Burns)

The San Wan — 1916   (courtesy of Rosario Resort)

when a masonry observation tower—constructed under state and federal auspices—was completed in 1940. Designed by Seattle architect Ellsworth Storey, the tower was patterned after ancient watch towers of the Caucasus Mountains of south-eastern Europe.

Moran's donation of the park, as well as the bridge and road improvements, came to over $90,000 of his own money for the public good.

The Sanwan

Not happy unless he was fulfilling his constructive tendencies, Robert Moran spent many hours at the machine shop. At one end of the building, where there was a variety of machinery representing an investment of many thousands of dollars, was his own private work shop. There he kept his pet tools in such order that he was able to locate them in the dark should his power plant be out of commission.

Moran spent several years building a 132 ft.

Four hundred guests were present at the launching of the San Wan — 1916.   (courtesy of Rosario Resort)

The launching of the Moran built San Wan.
(courtesy of Rosario Resort)

appropriate ceremony and a few short trips, the neglected yacht rocked gently at anchor on Cascade Bay.

> *When I again took up shipbuilding at Rosario, I built that fine yacht, Sanwan, as I thought for my own pleasure in its use. When I completed her, ready for sea, I put her to an anchor where she lay for years unused, while I proceeded on some other construction work on the land. When I planned and constructed the vessel, I thought it would be fine to go cruising over the waters of the world, but when she was finished, I found that my yacht building plans were a mistaken idea.*

The *Sanwan* was later turned over to Moran's son Frank, and used as a training ship in connection with his Moran School for Boys on Bainbridge Island and Atascadero, California. Frank ultimately sold the yacht, and unfortunately it went ashore at Santa Barbara, California. Frank happened to be driving north from his school, and arrived in Santa Barbara just as the tugs were pulling her off the shore and out to sea to burn and sink her.

The Moran Family

In 1930, Robert's wife Melissa was taken to a Seattle hospital with cancer, and died two years later. Oldest son John Malcolm Moran, after serving as his father's construction foreman at Rosario, headed the Moran Manufacturing Co., a Seattle manufacturing and machinery dealership. Second son Frank Goding Moran founded Lakeside School in Seattle and in 1914 established Moran

Festivities at launching of SAN WAN.
(courtesy of Rosario Resort)

yacht, the *Sanwan*, in which he planned to make long ocean voyages. This yacht was built on ways at Rosario from plans drawn by the owner. The ship gave him more joy in building than in use, for by the time it was launched he had lost interest in the sea. He hosted four hundred guests from Seattle for the launching in 1916, and after

(courtesy of Rosario Resort)

The Robert Moran Family.   (courtesy of Rosario Resort)

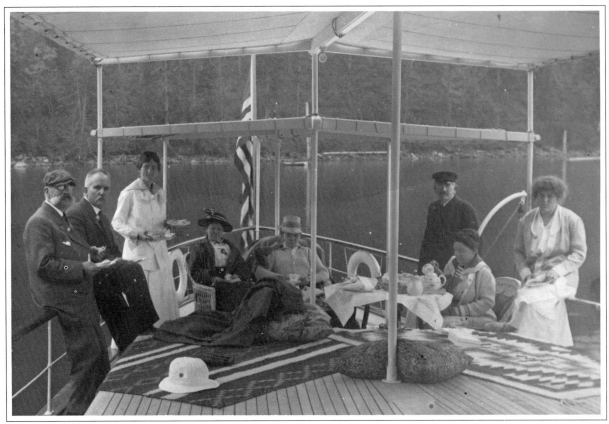

Afternoon cruise on Cascade Bay — Captain Tuttle and Robert Moran at left.   (courtesy of Rosario Resort)

School for Boys on Bainbridge Island, Washington and Atascadero, California, where he served as headmaster. Malcolm Edward Moran, the youngest son, served as a Sergeant of Field Artillery in France during World War I, where he was joined in the European war effort by adopted sister Mary Roberta Moran, who later married. Malcolm became an English and Physical Education instructor at the Moran School, and was also a successful freelance writer. Daughter Nellie Melissa Moran stayed on Orcas Island with her father.

Moran Sells Rosario

In 1932, Robert Moran had not only outlived his wife, but all of his brothers and sisters. Realizing his children's lost interest in the estate, and the demanded upkeep that he was no longer able to give it, he decided to sell Rosario.

I am now seventy-five years of age and my purpose in now offering the property for sale is to avoid passing it down to my descendants in a division of small stock interests, no one of which would be financially able to carry the expense of the occupancy or maintenance of the property. It is my desire that it be perpetuated as a whole, as, on account of water, power and other natural advantages, it can be more cheaply and advantageously operated in that manner.

The depression was at its worst, and even with large advertisements in *National Geographic* and *Fortune,* Moran had trouble selling. Naturally, the prospective buyer needed considerable means, but in such times the number of satisfactory offers were limited.

Moran published an album entitled *Rosario, an Estate in the Pacific Northwest,* promoting the property and island setting with detailed description and photographs of the estate. This volume was distributed to all major real estate companies in big cities across America. Finally, Rosario was sold in 1938 to a California industrialist named Donald Rheem. The purchase, which included 1339 acres, the fully furnished mansion and its surrounding homes and buildings, was for a mere $50,000!

Robert Moran, at eighty-one years of age, built a new home at White Beach near the ferry landing settlement of Orcas on the southwest side of the island. This home was nothing quite like Rosario, but it showed the same careful and painstaking planning and arrangement.

Moran took few of his possessions from Rosario to White Beach, but many diplomas and photographs of the *USS Nebraska* graced the walls, as well as a prized gun cabinet, with a shotgun, two rifles and several revolvers. But underneath, inscribed on a highly polished brass plate are the words: "NO KILLING OF WILDLIFE."

With no further construction plans for these properties, and realizing the uncertainty of life after eighty years of age, I sold Rosario and am now building a modest home on Orcas Island, where I am expecting to hold forth for many years to come.

A short time ago, I noticed a news item in a Bellingham paper to the effect that Moran had sold his palatial home, Rosario, and is now living in a forty year old shack formerly used as a cattle pen on Orcas Island. That is not literally true, as I am living in a building constructed by an Indian, when he homesteaded 160 acres on Orcas Island, now owned by my family. However, I have improved the old habitation to the extent that I have as good a bed and other conveniences, and sleep probably better than I did at Rosario. But the best of it all is that I am so constituted that it would be no burden for me to go back to life's conditions that were mine when I arrived in Seattle sixty-four years ago. That is more than would be agreeable to many of the rising generation. Money represented no value to me excepting as a means to carry on an industrious life on constructive lines. When I had money that I could not use in an industrial and constructive way, I gave it away. I got my pleasure out of a simple personal life by industry.

Ours was a family of twelve, ten children. I was the third on the birth calendar. The Creator seems to have reserved myself who proved to be the real father of the children during their lives in our State, to be the last one of the family to pass on.

Robert Moran died on March 27, 1943, at the age

Advertisement appearing in National Geographic Magazine — May 1933.
(courtesy of National Geographic Magazine)

Robert Moran's White Beach home, built in 1939.   (courtesy of Betty Moran Burns)

of eighty-six. He was a member of the Institute of Naval Architects, London; American Society of Naval Engineers; Franklin Institute; Pioneers Association of the State of Washington; and the Washington National Parks Association.

He was 'honorary member of the Northwest Society of Engineers, American Shipmasters Association and the Marine Engineer Association. He served two terms as Mayor of Seattle and during the war served the Governor for $1 a year as State Director of Public Service Reserve and Boy's Working Reserve.

The Rheems at Rosario

Donald Rheem, second owner of Rosario, was Chairman of the Board of the Rheem Manufacturing Company in California's Bay area. For twenty years Donald and his wife Alice used the estate as a part-time residence. Rheem often commuted from his California home by private amphibian plane, and built a concrete ramp to "drive" his plane onto the front lawn.

Alice Goodfellow Rheem was the daughter of a prominent international lawyer and California rancher and spent most of the year on Orcas Island. Her hobby was interior design and she was responsible for many improvements to the

mansion, such as additional oriental rugs and antique furniture. She was also responsible for changing the mansion's exterior from Moran's maroon to white.

Over $400,000 was spent on improvements and furnishings, including a $35,000 cabana, called the "Cliff House," which Mrs. Rheem had built one summer to show her husband she could successfully plan and supervise construction. It was rebuilt three times!

Donald Rheem was a very large shareholder at Paramount Studios in Hollywood, and built the Orinda and Rheem Theatres in California. An avid motion picture fan, he built a projection booth in the balcony of the music room, complete with two portable Simplex 35mm sound movie projectors. He also added a row of theatre seats in the balcony and a motor driven movie screen on the far wall. He would bring his many guests to the music room each evening after dinner to enjoy a newly released Paramount film. Rheem also built a concrete bulkhead and bandstand overlooking the Sound on the back lawn, where he would greet many of his guests arriving by boat with live band music.

The Rheems entertained friends often, yet the estate was kept more private than when Moran lived there. An iron gate was installed at the

(courtesy of Rosario Resort)

was in California, and her unusual appearances in the village of Eastsound wearing a flaming red nightgown, playing a few hands of cards with "local boys" at the general store, and hopping back on her motorcycle to get home! No doubt an eccentric character, she may well be why Donald bought an estate on an island so far from his bay area home.

Donald was the son of William S. Rheem, founder and Chairman of the Board of Standard Oil of California. During the family's twenty year ownership of Rosario many Standard Oil board meetings were held there.

Mrs. Rheem died at Rosario in 1956, and Donald sold the estate in 1958. However, many guests who have stayed there since 1958 have reported bizarre incidents, leading others to believe Mrs. Rheem's spirit still resides in the mansion!

Donald Rheem sold Rosario to Ralph Curton and the Falcon Corporation of Waco, Texas for a reported $455,000. Ralph Curton intended to use Rosario as the focal point of a planned resort residential development. A small amount of estate property was subdivided, and various original estate homes, such as the round house and two identical Moran brothers' homes, were sold to private owners. Curton's plans did not materialize, and the estate was again sold in 1960.

Rosario Resort

Rosario was purchased by Gilbert H. Geiser, former Mayor of Mountlake Terrace, Washington, for $225,000 — still completely furnished! The estate was opened as Rosario Resort by Mr. Geiser in June of 1960, thus continuing the tradition of fine hospitality in the Pacific Northwest that was started in 1905 by Robert Moran!

entrance bearing a no trespassing sign. With the Rheems keeping to themselves, curious Orcas Islanders often wondered what was happening at Rosario, and many colorful stories circulated. These stories were often fed by Mrs. Rheem's flamboyant lifestyle, including the hosting of armed services personnel while husband Donald

Acknowledgements

Many special thanks to the following: Sarah and Gilbert Geiser, Gerdta Foust and Manfred Cieslik, all of whom allowed me the opportunity to write this book; the Moran family — Betty and John Burns for sharing their family history and treasures, Mrs. Reeves (Patricia) Moran for so graciously sharing her late husband's family research and Malcolm Moran for his wonderful childhood stories; Joseph B. Stone, former Chairman of Communication Arts Department at Loyola/ Marymount University in Los Angeles for his editing of this project; Prof. William Holm of the University of Washington for his expertise in Chinook Jargon; and also thanks to the Museum of History and Industry, Whatcom County Museum, Seattle Public Library, University of Washington and Washington State Historical Society. Finally, I gratefully acknowledge Gary Smith and Jean Streinz of Adpro Litho for their involvement in designing and producing this book.

Humor was ever present in the brothers, erupting into tricks and "horseplay" aimed at each other or wives and children.   (courtesy of Rosario Resort)

Bibliography

Bagley, Clarence B. *History of Seattle from the Earliest Settlement to the Present time* (Chicago: S.J. Clark Publishing Co., 1916).

Coontz, Robert Edward. *From Mississippi to the Sea.* (Philadelphia: Dorrance and Co., Inc., 1930).

Hanford, Cornelius Holgate, *Seattle and Environs 1852-1924.* (Seattle: Pioneer Historical Publishing Co., 1924).

Meany, Edmond S. *Origin of Washington Geographic Names.* (University of Washington Press, 1923).

Moran, Robert. *An Address by Robert Moran at the Fiftieth Jubilee Meeting of The Pioneers Association of the State of Washington, June 6, 1939 in Seattle.* (Seattle: Copyright Malcolm E. Moran, 1939).

Moran, Robert. *Rosario, An estate in the Pacific Northwest.* (Undated, circa 1932).

Morgan, C.T. *The San Juan Story.* (Friday Harbor, WA: San Juan Industries, 1966).

Muir, John. *Travels in Alaska.* (Boston and New York: Houghton Mifflin Co., 1915).

Potter, Elisabeth Walton. *National Register of Historic Places — Nomination Form.* (United States Department of Interior/National Park Service, 1976).

Richardson, David. *Magic Islands.* (Eastsound, WA: Orcas Publishing Co., 1964).

Richardson, David. *Pig War Islands.* (Eastsound, WA: Orcas Publishing Co., 1971).

Speidel, William C. *Sons of the Profits.* (Seattle: Nettle Creek Publishing Co., 1967).

Splitstone, Fred John. *Orcas . . . the Gem of the San Juans.* (Bellingham, WA: Cox Brothers, 1946).

PERIODICALS: *The Sea Chest; Journal of the Puget Sound Maritime Historical Society; Railway and Marine News; The Craftsmen.*

NEWSPAPERS: *The Islands Sounder; The Journal of the San Juans; The Oregonian; The Orcas Islander; The Seattle Post-Intelligencer; The Seattle Star; The Seattle Times; The Tacoma News Tribune; The University of Washington Daily.*

ARCHIVAL COLLECTIONS: Betty Moran Burns Collection; Robert Moran Library at Rosario Resort; Museum of History and Industry; Seattle Public Library; Washington State Historical Society; and the University of Washington Northwest and Manuscript Collections.

Family members with domestic staff. Seattle 1903.
(courtesy of Whatcom Museum Archive)

The Moran Family — Robert Moran and wife Melissa (seated), John M., Nellie, adopted daughter Mary, Frank G. and Malcolm E. Moran.
(courtesy of Rosario Resort)